Lessons in Yeshua's Torah

First Edition Reader

Cover art by Lorie Hawkes

Written by Sarah Hawkes Valente

© 2022 WHATEVER IS LOVELY PUBLICATIONS LLC

Table of Contents:

Introduction	7
Genesis 1:1 - 6:8	9
Genesis 6:9 - 11:32	21
Genesis 12:1 - 17:27	30
Genesis 18:1 - 22:24	41
Genesis 23:1 - 25:18	53
Genesis 25:19 - 28:9	60
Genesis 28:10 - 32:2	69
Genesis 32:3 - 36:43	81
Genesis 37:1 - 40:23	90
Genesis 41:1 - 44:17	99
Genesis 44:18 - 47:27	110
Genesis 47:28 - 50:26	118

Exodus 1:1 - 6:1	126
Exodus 6:2 - 9:35	138
Exodus 10:1 - 13:16	148
Exodus 13:17 - 17:16	156
Exodus 18:1 - 20:23	166
Exodus 21:1 - 24:18	173
Exodus 25:1 - 27:19	185
Exodus 27:20 - 30:10	193
Exodus 30:11 - 34:35	201
Exodus 35:1 - 38:20	212
Exodus 38:21 - 40:38	212
Leviticus 1:1 - 5:26	221
Leviticus 6:1 - 8:36	228
Leviticus 9:1 - 11:47	236
Leviticus 12:1 - 13:59	243
Leviticus 14:1 - 15:33	243

Leviticus 16:1 - 18:30	253
Leviticus 19:1 - 20:27	253
Leviticus 21:1 - 24:23	263
Leviticus 25:1 - 26:2	271
Leviticus 26:3 - 27:34	271
Numbers 1:1 - 4:20	280
Numbers 4:21 - 7:89	291
Numbers 8:1 - 12:16	299
Numbers 13:1 - 15:41	306
Numbers 16:1 - 18:32	314
Numbers 19:1 - 22:1	321
Numbers 22:2 - 25:9	321
Numbers 25:10 - 30:1	336
Numbers 30:2 - 32:42	347
Numbers 33:1 - 36:13	347
Deuteronomy 1:1 - 3:22	359

Deuteronomy 3:23 - 7:11	367
Deuteronomy 7:12 - 11:25	375
Deuteronomy 11:26 - 16:17	382
Deuteronomy 16:18 - 21:9	390
Deuteronomy 21:10 - 25:19	398
Deuteronomy 26:1 - 29:8	408
Deuteronomy 29:9 - 30:20	418
Deuteronomy 31:1-30	418
Deuteronomy 32:1-52	425
Deuteronomy 33:1 - 34:12	430

Introduction

I began to read the Torah as a relevant portion of Scripture when I was thirty-three years old. I had read my Bible cover to cover many times, and for many years, before that. *Reading* Scripture is what good Christians do. But one afternoon, I sat in awe of King David's meditations, and something stirred in my spirit. David chased YHVH's heart by meditating on His Law. That wasn't something I knew how to do.

When I began reading through the weekly Torah Portions, my Bible study transformed. Quiet time morphed from something "done" to an incredible, heart-pounding journey. They were the same words I had read so many times before. Still, somehow, they weren't. My love of the *Old Testament* was new and precious, and my excitement for the *New Testament* was profound. That was more than a decade ago now, and every year since has been richly blessed.

Torah portions are an ancient tradition that began back in the time of Nehemiah and Ezra. When the Israelites returned from captivity, they wanted to make sure they didn't end up there again. They knew it was their disobedience that had gotten them into trouble. So, they created a weekly Torah reading schedule to make sure that everyone would hear the Torah read through once per year. This is the same schedule *Yeshua* (Jesus) followed when He walked the earth, and it's the same schedule followed today.

Each section of this book contains a detailed version of the Torah Portion that is specifically written for young readers. Also included are the haftarah readings, daily readings from the New Testament, and discussion questions.

My family and I believe that the Father and the Son are One. As James said, we truly believe there is **one** Lawgiver who is able to save. That's our *Yeshua*, and He is the Word of YHVH. It is my sincere hope that you will travel this road with us, day by day, as we grow closer to our Messiah.

B'resheet (In the beginning) – Genesis 1:1 - 6:8; Isaiah 42:5 - 43:10

Portion:

Part I: Genesis 1:1-26

NT: Colossians 1:3-17; John 1:1-14

God was there in the beginning, and He made the heavens and the earth. The earth was like a wasteland, and God's Spirit waited over the water. Everything was dark until God talked about light. He said, "Let light exist!" and then light existed. God made the first day and night by separating the light from the dark.

On the second day, God created an arch to separate the earth from the heavens. He called the arch the sky, and He divided the high waters above the sky from the waters down on Earth.

On the third day, God spoke to the oceans, and He told them to make room for dry land. When the land was ready, God planted trees and flowers and vegetables and fruit. If He said it, it came to life. He did all of that on the third day.

On the fourth day, God put the lights in the heavens. There was already light because God made it, but there was no shining sun or moon, and there were no stars, until God created them on the fourth day. God said that the sun, moon, and stars were made to tell us the time and to mark God's special days. They were also made to give light to everything on Earth.

On the fifth day, God spoke both to the waters and to the sky. He filled them with fish and birds.

On the sixth day, God filled the land with animals and insects. Then, finally, God made man. He said, "Let us make man in our image, so they may rule over this creation."

Discussion:

What did God make on each day?

On what day did God make fish, birds, man, etc.?

What did God create first, the light or the sun?

What times do the sun, moon, and stars tell us about?

Part II: Genesis 1:27-2:25

NT: Mark 10:1-9

On the sixth day, God created man in His own image; in the image of God He created them. He created them as male and female. He blessed them, and He told them to have children. "Fill the earth!" He said. He told them to rule over the creation.

Then God told man what He had given them for food: every plant that produces a seed and every tree whose fruit has seeds in it.

God saw everything He had made, and He saw that it was very good. This is how everything was made in six days. By the seventh day, God had finished. So, on the seventh day, He rested; He made the seventh day holy.

YHVH is God. He created the heavens and the earth. In the beginning of the world, God did not send any rain. A mist came up from the earth and watered the ground. When God made the first man, Adam, He made him from the dust of the ground. YHVH breathed life into Adam's nostrils, and Adam began to live.

God placed Adam in a beautiful garden that He had planted in Eden. A river flowed out of Eden, and it split into four rivers: the Pishon, the Gihon, the Tigris, and the Euphrates. God put Adam in charge of the Garden in Eden, and He told him to take care of it.

God made many wonderful things grow in the Garden in Eden, and there were two trees in the middle of the garden: the Tree of Life and the Tree of the Knowledge of Good and Evil. Adam could eat from the Tree of Life whose fruit made men live forever! But YHVH told Adam *never* to eat from the Tree of the Knowledge of Good and Evil. God gave Adam a very serious warning: *if* Adam ate from that forbidden tree, he would most definitely die.

Now every living creature was brought to Adam to see what he wanted to name it. Adam named them all. Every creature Adam named had a partner, but Adam was alone. He was lonely. God saw that this was not good, so He put Adam to sleep and took flesh and bone from his side. From the side of Adam, YHVH formed a woman. God gave this woman to Adam to be his wife. Adam called her "woman," because she was made from man. A husband and a wife become one person because woman was taken out of man.

Adam and his wife were naked, and they were not embarrassed.

Discussion:

What did God give man to eat?

What day did God make holy?

How did God make man?

From what tree was Adam warned never to eat?

What did God say would happen to Adam if he ate from the Tree of the Knowledge of Good and Evil?

From what tree did God want him to eat?

Where did Adam's wife come from?

Part III: Genesis 3:1-24

NT: Romans 5:12-17; Revelation 22:1-5

    The serpent was sneakier than any other creature. He came to the woman and asked her about the tree that grew in the middle of the garden: the Tree of the Knowledge of Good and Evil.

"Are you allowed to eat of all the fruit in this garden?" the serpent asked the woman. "Did God really say you can't have *all* of this good fruit?"

"We may eat from all except from this tree in the middle," the woman answered the snake. "If we eat from that one, we will die. We can't even touch it," she said.

"You will not die!" the serpent laughed at her. "God just wants to be smarter than you are. If you eat that fruit, you'll be like God!"

The woman took a bite from the fruit that God had told them never to eat. Adam stood beside her, and she handed the fruit to him. He took a bite of it, too.

Adam and his wife were immediately ashamed. They knew they'd disobeyed God, and they were scared and embarrassed. They knew that they were naked. They hid in the bushes and tried to cover their bodies. YHVH knew what they had done, and He came to find them there.

"Where are you?" He called to Adam.

"I heard You in the garden, and I hid because I'm naked."

"Who told you that you were naked? Did you eat the fruit I commanded you not to eat?"

Adam answered and said, "The woman that You put here with me—she gave it to me, and I ate it."

YHVH said to the woman, "What have you done?"

"The snake tricked me into eating it!" she said.

YHVH cursed the snake because of what it had done to the woman. He said, "You will crawl on your belly and eat dust forever. Your children and the woman's children will be enemies. Her Child will crush your head, and you will strike His heel."

To the woman, YHVH said, "Giving birth to children will be very painful for you. You will long for your husband, and he will rule over you."

YHVH said to Adam, "Because you listened to your wife instead of to Me, the ground is cursed because of you. You will have to pull out thorns and thistles before you can plant and harvest; your work will be very hard. You were made from dust, and you will return to dust again."

Adam named his wife *Chavvah*, meaning "life," because she would be the mother of all people.

YHVH made clothes of skin for Adam and his wife. He said, "Man has become like one of us, knowing good from evil. If we leave him here, he will eat from the Tree of Life and live forever."

So YHVH forced Adam and Chavvah to leave the garden. He left cherubim with a flaming sword to guard the Tree of Life.

Discussion:

Did God tell Adam and his wife that they were not allowed to touch the Tree of the Knowledge of Good and Evil?

When the woman told the serpent what God had said, what did the serpent say?

What happened to Adam and his wife because of their disobedience?

Sometimes we call Adam's wife Eve. What was her Hebrew name? What does it mean?

Part IV: Genesis 4:1-26

NT: Hebrews 11:3-4; I John 3:11-13

Adam and Chavvah had many children. Their first two sons were named Cain and Abel. Cain became a farmer, and Abel became a shepherd. When it was time to bring sacrifices to God, Cain brought some of his harvest. Abel brought fat portions from the first-born of his livestock. God was not happy with Cain or his offering, and this made Cain very angry. Abel had done right, and God was happy with Abel. This made Cain mad at Abel, too. YHVH warned Cain about his anger, but Cain did not listen.

Cain invited his brother to go with him into the field. While they were there, Cain attacked Abel and killed him.

"Where is Abel?" YHVH asked Cain.

"I don't know; he's not my responsibility," Cain answered.

"I can hear your brother's blood crying from the ground!

You are under a curse; you must leave here and wander the earth."

Cain said, "This is too harsh! Whoever finds me will kill me."

YHVH put a mark on Cain so that whoever found him would not kill him. YHVH said, "Anyone who kills Cain will suffer seven times worse."

So, Cain left and lived in Nod.

Cain and his wife had a son named Enoch. Enoch was the father of Mahujael. Mahujael was the father of Methushael. Methushael was the father of Lamech. Lamech had two wives. Adah was the mother of Jabel and Jubal. Zillah was the mother of Tubal-Cain.

One day, Lamech killed a man who had wounded him. Lamech said to his wives, "If Cain's killer would be paid back seven times, then anyone who kills me should be paid back seventy times!"

Adam and Chavvah had another son, and they named him Seth. They said, "God has given us this son in place of Abel because Cain killed him." Later, Seth had a son who he named him Enosh. At this time, people began to call on the name of YHVH.

Discussion:

Which of Adam's first sons became a shepherd?

Which son was a farmer?

Why do you think God was not happy with Cain's offering?

When Cain saw that God was not happy, what should he have done?

What did Cain do?

Why do you think Cain was mad at Abel? Have you ever been angry at someone for doing right?

Part V: Genesis 5:1-6:8

NT: Jude; Luke 3:23-38

When God created mankind, He created them in His image. He created them as male and female, and He blessed them and named them Adam.

Adam was 130 years old when Seth was born. Adam had many other children, and he died when he was 930 years old.

Seth was 105 when Enosh was born. Seth had many other children, and he died when he was 912 years old.

Enosh was 90 when Kenan was born. Enosh had many other children, and he died when he was 905 years old.

Kenan was 70 when Mahalalel was born. Kenan had many other children, and he died when he was 910 years old.

Mahalalel was 65 when Jared was born. Mahalalel had many other children, and he died when he was 830 years old.

Jared was 162 when Enoch was born. Jared had many other children, and he died when he was 800 years old.

Enoch was 65 when Methuselah was born. Enoch had many other children. Enoch walked with God, and then God took him away when he was 365 years old.

Methuselah was 187 when Lamech was born. Methuselah had many other children, and he died when he was 969 years old.

Lamech was 182 when Noah was born. Lamech had many other children, and he died when he was 777 years old.

After Noah was 500 years old, he became the father of Shem, Ham, and Japheth.

When there were many human beings on Earth, the sons of God saw the daughters of men and took them as their wives. YHVH said, "My Spirit will not remain in humans forever; they are not immortal. They will have one hundred and twenty years."

There were giants on Earth, then and later, because the sons of god had children with the daughters of men.

YHVH saw how wicked the people had become. They only thought evil thoughts and

only wanted evil things. God wished He had never made man, and He decided to destroy them. But YHVH was happy with Noah.

Discussion:

Why did YHVH decide to destroy the people that He had made?

Noach (Noah) –
Genesis 6:9 - 11:32; Isaiah 52:13 - 55:5

Portion:

Part I: Genesis 6:9-22

NT: Matthew 24; Luke 17:26-37

Noah walked with God even though the people of his time did not. Noah had three sons: Shem, Ham, and Japheth.

God saw that the people of Earth were corrupt. He told Noah about His plan. He said, "The earth is filled with violence because the people are so wicked. I am going to destroy them. Build a big boat, an ark, out of gopherwood. Make rooms inside of the boat, and coat the inside and outside with tar. The ark should be three hundred cubits long, fifty cubits wide, and thirty cubits high: three stories. Put a roof on top and a door in the side. I am going to bring a flood that will destroy everything on Earth, but I will create My covenant with you. You will enter the ark with your wife, your sons, and your sons' wives. You must take two of every creature inside with you, male and female, to keep them alive. You must gather every kind of food and store it to feed both you and the animals."

Noah obeyed God.

Discussion:

Why did God decide to destroy man? How was God going to do this?

How tall was Noah's ark?

Part II: Genesis 7:1-8:12

NT: Hebrews 11:6-7; I Peter 3:18-22

YHVH said to Noah, "Get in the ark with your family. You are righteous in My eyes;

you are not like your generation. Take one pair (a male and female) of every unclean animal and seven pairs of every clean animal with you. Also, take seven pairs of every kind of bird. In seven days, I will send rain. I will wash every other living thing from the earth."

Noah obeyed YHVH.

Noah was six hundred years old when the flood came. On the seventeenth day of the second month, Noah and his family entered the ark. The animals came to Noah because YHVH sent them. YHVH shut them into the ark. On the same day, God ripped open the sky and cracked the earth so that water gushed from overhead and from underneath. Rain beat upon the earth for forty days and nights! The waters rose, covering the mountains, and the ark floated high above the earth. Everything outside the ark died.

God remembered Noah, and He sent a strong wind to dry out the land. It took one hundred and fifty days for the water to begin to go down. On the seventeenth day of the seventh month, the ark landed on the mountains of Ararat. On the first day of the tenth month, the tops of the mountains of Ararat could finally be seen again.

After forty days, Noah sent a raven and a dove through a window in the ark. The raven flew back and forth, waiting for the ground to dry. The dove returned to the ark because it found no place to land. A week later, Noah sent the dove out again; this time it returned with an olive leaf in its mouth. Noah knew that life was beginning! After another week he sent the dove out again. This time, it did not return; it had found plenty to eat and places to rest on the earth.

Discussion:

Did Noah know the difference between clean and unclean animals?

How many days did the rain fall? What did God send to dry out the rain?

On what mountains did the ark land?

How many times did Noah send out the dove?

How/why did the raven and the dove have different needs?

Part III: Genesis 8:13-9:17

NT: II Peter 2:4-9

Noah removed the covering from the ark on the first day of the first month. He was six hundred and one years old. By the twenty-seventh day of the second month, over one year after entering the ark, the ground was completely dry. God told Noah to bring his family and animals out of the ark. God commanded them to have children and to once again fill the earth.

When Noah left the ark, he built an altar to YHVH. He sacrificed some of the clean animals to God. When God smelled the sacrifice, He was pleased. God promised to never again destroy the whole earth with a flood. Then God blessed Noah and his sons. "Have children and fill the earth," He said. "The animals will be afraid of you; I give them to you for food just like I gave you the green plants. But do not eat meat that still has its blood in it."

Because of the violence on the earth before the flood, God told Noah that there would now be a punishment for murder: life for life. No one could take a life on purpose without their life being taken in return, because mankind was created in the image of God.

God said, "This is My covenant promise to you and to every creature that was inside the ark: I will never again destroy the whole earth with a flood. As a sign of this covenant between you and Me, I put My bow in the sky. When I bring clouds and the rainbow appears, I will remember My promise to you."

Discussion:

How long were Noah and his family inside the ark?

What did Noah do when he left the ark?

What promise did God make to Noah? What was/is the sign of this promise?

What do you think life was like after the flood? Can you imagine your family being the only people on Earth?

Part IV: Genesis 9:18-10:32

NT: Ephesians 6:1-9

[Mature content ahead.]

The three sons of Noah were Shem, Ham, and Japheth. All the people on Earth were born from Noah's three sons and their wives.

Noah was a farmer, and he planted a vineyard. When his grapes were grown and his wine was ready, Noah became drunk in his tent. One night, Noah fell asleep undressed, and Ham came in and saw him. Ham thought his father's embarrassment was funny, and he brought his brothers to laugh at their father. Shem and Japheth would not laugh, however. They carried a blanket and walked backwards to cover their father. Then they left Noah alone in his tent.

When Noah realized what Ham had done, he became very angry. Noah cursed Ham by cursing Ham's son, Canaan. Noah blessed Shem and Japheth, and he said that Canaan would be Shem's slave.

After the flood, Japheth had seven sons: Gomer, Magog, Madai, Javan, Tubal, Meshek, and Tiras. His sons also had sons of their own.

Ham had four sons: Cush, Egypt, Put, and Canaan. Cush was the father of Nimrod who became a mighty warrior in the face of God and built the city of Nineveh. Egypt became the father of the Philistines. Canaan became the father of the Hittites, Jebusites, Amorites, and Hivites.

Shem had five sons: Elam, Ashur, Arphaxad, Lud, and Aram.

Discussion:

Which son dishonored his father?

Who did Noah curse? Who did Noah bless?

Why do you think Noah cursed Canaan instead of Ham? Were Ham's other sons blessed?

Part V: Genesis 11:1-32

NT: Matthew 1

Noah's now very large family all spoke one language; they moved together and camped near each other. When they arrived at a land called Shinar, they decided to build a city. In the city, they began to build a tower; they wanted that tower to reach toward the heavens so that they would be famous for building it.

When God saw the people working together, He knew they could accomplish their goal. To keep this from happening, He confused their languages. Because of this, the tower was called Babble. God confused their languages, and He scattered the people across the earth.

This is the family line from Shem to Abram:

Shem was the father of Arphaxad.

Arphaxad was the father of Shelah.

Shelah was the father of Eber.

Eber was the father of Peleg.

Peleg was the father of Reu.

Reu was the father of Serug.

Serug was the father of Nahor.

Nahor was the father of Terah.

Terah was the father of Abram, Nahor, and Haran; Haran was the father of Lot. Terah died in the land of Ur while his father was still alive. Abram married Sarai, and Nahor married Milkah. Abram and Sarai did not have any children because she was not able to get pregnant.

Haran died while they were still living in Ur. Then Terah, Abram, Sarai, and Lot all traveled together toward the land of Canaan. When they arrived in a place called Haran (this is the same name as Abram's brother who had died), they stopped there. They settled in Haran, and Terah died there when he was two hundred and five years old.

Discussion:

The people were all working together. Why did God not like this?

To keep them from accomplishing their goal, what did God do?

Lech Lecha (Get yourself out) –
Genesis 12:1 - 17:27; Isaiah 40:27 - 41:16

Portion:

Part I: Genesis 12:1-20

NT: Galatians 3:28-29

Abram had traveled from Ur with his father's family. God told Abram to leave his father's family and to travel to a faraway land that He would show him. God did not tell Abram much about the journey, but He did tell him three big things: God promised to make Abram's family a great nation, God promised to bless Abram, and God promised to bless the people of the whole earth through Abram.

When he was seventy-five years old, after his father had died in Haran, Abram did what God had told him to do. Abram packed his bags, and Sarai and Abram left Haran heading toward the land of Canaan. Abram did not leave behind *all* his father's family. Abram's nephew, Lot, came along.

God led Abram to a place called Shechem in the land of Canaan. The Canaanites were living there. Still, God appeared to

Abram and told him that this land would belong to his family. Abram built an altar in Shechem because God appeared to him there. Then Abram traveled to Bethel. He built an altar in Bethel as well.

Abram didn't stay long in Canaan. There was no rain, and crops would not grow. People were starving. Because there was food in Egypt, Abram left Canaan and traveled there.

When Abram and his family were about to enter the strange land of Egypt, Abram became afraid. His wife, Sarai, was a very beautiful woman. Abram was afraid that an Egyptian would see her and would want her to be his wife. Abram worried the Egyptians would kill him just so that Sarai would be free to marry. Abram had an idea; he asked Sarai to say that she was his sister. If she was only his sister, and not his wife, then the Egyptians would treat Abram well and his life would not be in danger.

Sarai did as Abram said. Just as Abram feared, the Egyptians did notice Sarai. They told the king about Sarai, and he wanted to marry her. He gave Abram, who he thought was her brother, many animals and servants as gifts. Then Pharaoh took Sarai into the palace to be his wife.

Sarai obeyed her husband, and God protected her. God sent terrible diseases to the palace. Pharaoh and his household became very sick because Sarai was there. Soon Pharaoh realized that he had been tricked, and he called Abram to the palace. Pharaoh sent Sarai back to her husband and told them to leave Egypt right away. Abram was allowed to keep all of the animals and servants that the king had given him. They left Egypt as rich people.

Discussion:

Who did God tell Abram to leave behind?

Did Abram obey God?

Why did Abram tell Sarai to lie?

What would have happened to Sarai if Abram had been killed?

What happened to Pharaoh while Sarai was in his palace?

How did Abram and Sarai become rich in Egypt?

Part II: Genesis 13:1-18

NT: Galatians 3:1-30

After leaving Egypt, Abram, Sarai, and Lot went back and camped between Bethel and Ai. This time, the land was not big enough for all their new things, servants, and animals. Lot and Abram fought, and their servants fought, because the land was crowded.

Abram didn't want to fight with his nephew. He asked Lot to pick the land he wanted. If Lot chose to go right, Abram would go left. Then there would be enough room for both families. Lot looked to the east, and he chose the very green and beautiful land around the Jordan. This is where the cities of Sodom and Gomorrah were. Lot camped near Sodom, and Abram lived in Canaan.

Once Lot was gone, God told Abram to look around. God told him to look north, south, east, and west. All of the land Abram saw was his. God told him so. God was giving it to him and to his seed forever. God told Abram to walk the land. Abram did, and then he camped at Hebron and built an altar to YHVH.

Discussion:

Why do you think God told Abram to look around at the land *after* Lot had left?

Part III: Genesis 14:1-24

NT: Hebrews 7:1-10

During this time, four kings from the east were at war with five kings of Canaan. King Kedorlaomer was the leader of the four mighty kings. These four kings conquered people after people. Then they conquered Sodom and Gomorrah. When the four kings of the east attacked Sodom, they took Lot and his family prisoner (as well as the other citizens of Sodom and Gomorrah). They also took the wealth of Sodom and Gomorrah and all of the food that was there.

A man who escaped from the battle ran to Abram to tell him the news. Abram hurried to rescue Lot. Abram had many servants now, and in his household were three hundred and eighteen men who were trained for battle. Abram took his trained men and followed Kedorlaomer and the mighty kings' armies. With God's help, Abram's small army defeated the four mighty kings. Abram rescued Lot and the rest of the captured people. He also brought back the riches that Kedorlaomer's army had taken.

When Abram returned from battle, two men met with him in the Valley of Shaveh. This valley is called the King's Valley. Melchizedek, a priest of God, brought bread and wine to Abram. Melchizedek blessed Abram. He told Abram he was blessed by God, and he praised God for allowing Abram's small army to defeat Kedorlaomer's army. God had fought for Abram! Abram gave Melchizedek a tenth of everything.

The king of Sodom also met with Abram. He was very grateful to Abram, and he offered to let Abram keep all of the riches that he'd brought back from the war. Abram was a wealthy man, but this would have made Abram as wealthy as a king!

Abram told the king of Sodom that he could not accept Sodom's riches. "I promised God I would not take anything from you," Abram said. "You won't be the one to make me rich."

Discussion:

How many soldiers did Abram have?

How many kings' armies was Abram fighting against?

What did the king of Sodom offer to Abram?

Part IV: Genesis 15:1-21

NT: Luke 1:46-55; Acts 3:25-26

After Abram turned down the offer from the king of Sodom, YHVH spoke to him. He said, "Don't be afraid, Abram. I am your protection. I am the One who provides for you. I am the One who makes you rich."

Abram reminded God that He still hadn't given him a child. Abram and his wife were old, and they didn't think they'd have children now. But God told Abram to look at the stars. "Can you count the stars, Abram?" God said. "This is how many children, grandchildren, and great-grandchildren you will have. You won't even be able to count them! This land that I brought you to will be yours and your children's forever!"

Abram believed what YHVH said. God was very happy with Abram's faith. Then Abram asked for a sign between him and YHVH, so God told Abram to bring a cow, a goat, a ram, a dove, and a pigeon. Except for the birds, which he left whole, Abram cut the animals into two pieces. He arranged the halves on the ground so there was a path of blood between them. Birds came to try and eat the dead animals, but Abram scared them away.

At sunset, Abram fell into a kind of trance. YHVH spoke to him and said, "Your children will be slaves in a foreign land. Then, I will rescue them. You will not be a slave, though. You will live a long and good life. Your children will come back to this land and defeat the Amorites, but it is not time to destroy them yet."

When it was dark, a smoking pot and a burning torch went through the bloody path that had formed between the halves of the animals. YHVH made a covenant with Abram, and He said, "To you and your children, I give all this land from the river of Egypt to the Euphrates. The Kenites, Kenizzites, Kadmonites, Hittites, Perizzites, Rephaites, Amorites, Canaanites, Girgashites, and Jebusites live there now."

Discussion:

Why didn't God want Abram to accept the wealth of Sodom?

Why did fire *and* smoke pass between the cut animals?

Part V: Genesis 16:1-17:27

NT: Romans 4; Colossians 2:11-15

Ten years after leaving Haran and arriving in Canaan, Abram and Sarai still did not have a child. They began to worry. God had promised to make Abram a great nation, and they believed Him. But after ten years, they were tired of waiting. Sarai was too old to have children now, and Sarai's servant was much younger than she was. So, Sarai asked Abram to marry her Egyptian servant and to have a child with her instead.

Abram agreed, and he married Hagar. When Hagar became pregnant, she began to disrespect Sarai since Sarai had never had any children. This bothered Sarai, and Sarai began to hate Hagar. She treated Hagar very badly, and Hagar ran away.

The angel of YHVH found Hagar and told her to go back to Sarai. He told her that her son would be born and that her descendants would be too many to count. He told her that her son's name would be Ishmael and that he would fight with his brothers. Everyone would be against him, and he would be against everyone. Hagar called YHVH "The God who sees me." She went back to Sarai and gave birth to the baby. Abram named him Ishmael.

Fourteen years later, YHVH came and talked to Abram. He told him to be perfect and to obey His commandments. Again, YHVH said He would make Abram a great nation. And again, God promised Abram the land. YHVH said, "Your name is now Abraham because you will be the father of many nations. There will be kings in your family. I will keep My covenant with all of your generations. I will be the God of your descendants, and I will give the whole land of Canaan to your family forever."

God gave Abraham the sign of the covenant. He said, "You must keep My covenant. Every male child in your household must be circumcised when he is eight days old—whether he is a natural born child, an adopted child, or a servant bought with money." Then God said, "Your wife, Sarai, is now named Sarah. She will give you a son. I will make her the mother of nations."

Abraham said, "We are so old! Can't you bless us through Ishmael instead?"

God said, "I will make great nations from both Hagar's son and Sarah's son. The covenant, though, will be through Sarah's son, Isaac. Sarah will give birth to Isaac by this time next year."

That same day, Abraham, Ishmael, and every male in Abraham's household was circumcised. Abraham was ninety-nine, and Ishmael was thirteen.

Discussion:

Why did Abram marry Hagar? Did God tell Abram to marry Hagar?

Do you think that God meant to make Abram a great nation through Hagar's child?

Who is the son God promised to Abram?

Would Ishmael be a great nation?

Vayera (He appeared) – Genesis 18:1 - 22:24; II Kings 4:1-37

Portion:

Part I: Genesis 18:1-33

NT: Luke 1:5-7

It was a hot afternoon. Abraham was sitting in the doorway of his tent. He looked up and saw three men standing nearby, but these were not ordinary men. When Abraham saw them, he ran to them and bowed. He said, "Please, YHVH, stay and wash Your feet! I will get You something to eat and drink!"

The men told him that they would stay. Abraham ran to have lunch prepared and to have his wife, Sarah, make some bread. When lunch was ready, he took it to the men. Abraham stood near them while they ate.

Sarah didn't come out of the tent. The men asked Abraham where she was because they'd come with news for her. Abraham told the men where she was, and then one of the men said, "I will return again about this same time next year; Sarah will have a son."

When Sarah heard the man say that she was going to have a baby, she couldn't help but laugh. She thought, *Now that I'm so old, and my husband is so old…now I will have a child?* The idea seemed silly to her.

Then YHVH said, "Why did Sarah just laugh?"

Sarah was afraid, and she answered back, "I didn't!" But God said, "Oh, yes you did."

When the men had finished eating, they got up to leave; Abraham walked with them. They looked toward Sodom where Lot lived. YHVH said, "Should I tell Abraham what I'm about to do? Abraham will be a great nation. I have chosen him; he keeps the ways of YHVH." Then YHVH said that He was going to Sodom to see the people's wickedness for Himself. He said, "Then I will know if their sin is as terrible as I have heard." Afterward, two of the men headed for Sodom leaving Abraham alone with YHVH.

When Abraham heard that God was planning to destroy Sodom, he immediately worried about his nephew, Lot. He asked God, "Will You let the good die with the wicked? What if there are fifty people there who know You and love You? Will You save the whole town if there are fifty righteous people?"

God answered Abraham and said, "Yes, if there are fifty, I will not destroy it."

Abraham wasn't sure there would be fifty godly people in a town as bad as Sodom. Abraham thought, and then he said, "What if there are forty-five people who know You and love You in Sodom? Will You save the whole town if there are forty-five righteous people?"

Again, God answered Abraham and said, "Yes, if there are forty-five, I will not destroy it."

Abraham continued to ask God this same question. The numbers grew smaller and smaller until Abraham finally asked God, "What about just ten people, YHVH? Will You save the whole town for only ten godly people?"

YHVH answered, "Yes, I will save it for ten." Then YHVH left Abraham, and Abraham went back home.

Discussion:

How many men came to see Sarah and Abraham that day?

Who do you think these men were?

What did the men tell Abraham?

How did Sarah react?

Why did God hesitate before telling Abraham about His plans to destroy Sodom?

How many righteous people would have to be found in Sodom before God would spare the town?

Part II: Genesis 19:1-38

NT: Matthew 10:30-42

When the two messengers arrived in Sodom, they saw that things were just as bad as they'd heard. They found Lot sitting near the gates of the city. When Lot saw them, he bowed. Lot invited the messengers to his house because the city was dangerous at night, and when night came, the men of Sodom surrounded Lot's house. They wanted to attack the strangers they had seen with Lot earlier that day.

Lot protected his guests, and the men of Sodom became angry at Lot. When the men tried to break down Lot's door, Lot's guests made the men of Sodom go blind.

Then the two guests said to Lot, "Hurry! Get anyone who belongs to you and take them out of this city. It is going to be destroyed!"

Lot believed the messengers, and he ran to warn the men who were engaged to marry his two daughters. His sons-in-law wouldn't listen, though. They thought he was only joking. Again, the messengers told Lot it was time to go, and this time they said to go *now*. When Lot seemed unsure, the messengers grabbed his hand and the hands of his wife and two daughters. They led them out of the city. They warned them to flee and to not look back.

When Lot and his family were safely away from Sodom, God rained burning sulfur from the heavens to destroy both Sodom and Gomorrah. Lot and his daughters were saved because God knew how much it meant to Abraham. Lot's wife disobeyed and looked back toward Sodom, and she was turned into a pillar of salt.

When Abraham woke in the morning, he went back to the place where he had talked with YHVH. He looked toward Sodom, and he saw a thick cloud of smoke rising from the ground. He knew that Sodom had been destroyed.

[Mature content ahead.]

When Lot ran from Sodom, he went to Zoar. But he was afraid to stay in Zoar, so he hid with his daughters in a cave. His daughters wanted to have children. They were afraid they never would because there weren't any men around them, so they tricked their father and gave him wine to drink. Then they each conceived a child with him. From these two children came the Ammonites and the Moabites.

Discussion:

Why did Lot bow when he saw the messengers?

What did the messengers do to the men when they tried to break down Lot's door?

Did Lot's whole family leave with him?

Did Lot want to leave Sodom?

What happened to Lot's wife?

Why did God rescue Lot from Sodom, even though he knew that Lot would father two ungodly nations?

Part III: Genesis 20:1-18

NT: I Peter 3:5-7; Matthew 5:43-48

Abraham moved from place to place. For a little while, he stayed in Gerar. When Abimelek, the king of Gerar, saw Sarah, he wanted her to be his wife. Abraham was afraid that the king would kill him and take his wife. Just like he had done in Egypt, Abraham told Abimelek that Sarah was his sister.

Abimelek took Sarah to live with him in his palace, but God did not let Abimelek touch her. Then one night God came to Abimelek in a dream. God warned the king that he was in danger of death because he had taken a married woman. He also told Abimelek that Sarah's husband, Abraham, was a prophet. Abimelek was very afraid. He hadn't meant to do anything wrong, and he hadn't known Sarah was married.

Abimelek asked Abraham why he had tricked him in such a horrible way. Abraham told him that he had been afraid because he didn't think the people of Gerar feared God. He also explained that Sarah was his half-sister (the daughter of his father but not his mother).

Abimelek told Abraham that he was free to live anywhere in his land. He gave Abraham servants and animals and a thousand silver coins to pay for any embarrassment he had caused Sarah.

Abraham prayed to God and asked Him to heal Abimelek; God had not let any of the king's wives become pregnant while Sarah was in Abimelek's house. When Abraham prayed, the king's family was healed.

Discussion:

Why did Abraham lie to Abimelek?

What did Abraham say was his reason for lying?

Part IV: Genesis 21:1-34

NT: Galatians 4:21-31

Just like God had said, Sarah had a son. Abraham named him Isaac. He circumcised the boy when he was eight days old—just as YHVH had commanded. Sarah was ninety years old when Isaac was born, and Abraham was one hundred. Sarah was so happy to be a mother; she said that God had made her laugh with happiness!

One day, when Isaac was old enough to eat solid food instead of his mother's milk, Abraham and Sarah threw him a big party. Sarah saw Hagar's son, Ishmael, laughing and making fun of Isaac. Sarah was very upset. Sarah told Abraham to send Hagar and Ishmael far away. Abraham loved Ishmael, so this made him very sad.

When Abraham asked God what he should do, God told him to listen to Sarah. God told him not to worry about Ishmael—that He would take care of him and make him a nation just like He had said. It was Isaac, however, who would become the promised nation.

Abraham packed food and water and sent Hagar and Ishmael away. They wandered out into the desert of Beersheba. When all their food and water was gone, Hagar put Ishmael under a bush. She walked away until he was just out of sight. She did not want to watch her son die, and she had nothing left to give him.

God had mercy on Hagar and Ishmael, and He spoke to Hagar as she sat listening to her son cry. God said, "Lift up your son, and don't be afraid. I will make him a great nation." Then God showed Hagar a well of water, and Hagar and Ishmael drank. They lived in the desert, and Ishmael became a bow hunter. When it was time for Ishmael to marry, Hagar found him a wife from Egypt.

Abraham still lived on Abimelek's land, and Abimelek came to Abraham and asked him to make a promise. "I have been kind to you," Abimelek said. "Please promise me that you will always be kind to my descendants." Abraham said, "I promise."

Then Abraham told Abimelek about a well of water that had been stolen from him. "I dug the well, and your servants took it over," Abraham said. Abimelek was shocked that this had happened, and he promised he hadn't known. Abraham brought sheep and cattle to Abimelek, and Abraham and Abimelek made a covenant. Abimelek believed that Abraham had dug the well, and he returned the well to Abraham. Abraham planted a tamarisk tree in the name of YHVH, and he lived in that land, which was the land of the Philistines, for a long time.

Discussion:

Why was Sarah upset with Ishmael?

Did Abraham want to send Ishmael away?

What happened when Hagar ran out of water?

What did Abimelek want Abraham to promise him?

What did Abraham tell Abimelek had been stolen from him?

Part V: Genesis 22:1-24

NT: Hebrews 11:13-19; James 2:21-24

After a while, God came to Abraham with a big test. God said, "Go to Moriah, and sacrifice Isaac on a mountain that I will show you."

Early the next morning, Abraham loaded his donkey. He took Isaac, some supplies, and two of his servants, and he went to obey the Lord.

On their third day of traveling, Abraham saw the place that God had told him about. He told his servants to stay behind with the donkey, and he took Isaac and the firewood up the mountain. Abraham also took a knife and a branch with a flame of fire, but Isaac noticed that his father had forgotten to bring a lamb. He said, "Father, where is the lamb for the sacrifice?"

Abraham answered, "Don't worry, son. The Lord will provide a lamb."

When they got to the right place, Abraham built an altar. He put wood on the altar, and then he tied Isaac on top. With the knife in his hand, Abraham raised his hand to kill Isaac. God saw that Abraham had passed the test. The Angel of YHVH said, "Stop! Don't hurt the boy! Now I know that you do not love or fear anyone more than Me." Abraham saw a ram caught in a bush, and he knew that God had provided a sacrifice. Abraham called the place, "YHVH will provide."

God said, "I swear by Myself, because you have obeyed Me, I will make your children as many as the sand of the seas. All the earth will be blessed through you because you have obeyed Me."

Awhile later, Abraham heard that his brother Nahor's wife, Milkah, had given birth to eight sons. He also heard that Nahor had four more sons with his concubine, Reumah.

Discussion:

What did God ask Abraham to do?

Was Abraham willing to obey?

What did Abraham sacrifice on the mountain?

Chayei Sarah (Sarah's life) – Genesis 23:1 - 25:18; I Kings 1:1-31

Portion:

Part I: Genesis 23:1-20

NT: Matthew 13:44-46; I Corinthians 15:41-43

Sarah lived to be one hundred and twenty-seven years old. Isaac was thirty-seven years old when she died. Sarah died in Hebron were she and Abraham had lived. After taking Isaac to sacrifice him on Mount Moriah, Abraham stayed in Beersheba. When Abraham heard that Sarah had died, he was very sad; he went to bury her. A wealthy Hittite named Ephron owned a piece of land with a cave that was a perfect burial place. Abraham wanted to bury Sarah in that cave, so he asked to buy the land. Ephron tried to give him the land because Abraham was a respected man, but Abraham insisted on buying it. He gave Ephron the full price of four hundred shekels of silver. After buying the land from Ephron, Abraham buried Sarah in that cave in the field of Machpelah near Mamre.

Discussion:

How old was Sarah when she died? Where was she buried?

Why was it important to Abraham that he pay for the land where Sarah was buried?

Part II: Genesis 24:1-9

NT: II Corinthians 6:14-18

Abraham was old, and he didn't want to die without knowing that Isaac would be married to a good woman from his family. So, Abraham called for the most important servant in his house. Abraham asked his servant to make him a promise. He said, "I do not want my son to marry anyone from Canaan. Travel back to the land where I was born and choose a wife for Isaac from my relatives."

"What if the young woman will not come back with me?" his servant asked.

"God will send an angel ahead of you to help you, but even if the young woman will not come back with you, do not take Isaac to Ur. This is the land YHVH is giving to us."

Discussion:

Why didn't Abraham want Isaac to marry a woman from Canaan?

Why didn't Abraham want Isaac to leave Canaan to find a wife?

Part III: Genesis 24:10-27

NT: Matthew 7:7-8

Abraham's most trusted servant, along with other servants, loaded ten camels with very nice gifts. Then they traveled to Abraham's homeland to find a wife for Isaac from Abraham's family. When they arrived in Nahor's town, they stopped by a water well. It was almost dinner time: the time of day when the women came to get water for cooking and washing. Abraham's servant stood by the well and prayed. He asked God to show him which woman was meant for Isaac. He told YHVH that he would ask a woman for water, and if she answered, "I will give you water, and I will get water for your camels, too," then he would know that she was the one God had chosen.

Before he had even finished praying, a beautiful young woman named Rebekah came to the well with a water jar on her shoulder. Abraham's servant asked her for water, and she answered, "I will give you water, and I will get water for your camels, too." The servant watched her as she carried jar after jar of water—enough to water ten thirsty camels! He was so impressed with her that he took jewelry from his bag to give to her. He asked her who she was, and she said, "I am Nahor and Milkah's granddaughter: Bethuel's daughter. We have feed and straw for your camels and a place for you to spend the night."

The servant was so happy that he bowed down and worshipped YHVH.

Discussion:

What did Abraham's servant pray as he stood by the well?

Who was Rebekah? Was she part of Abraham's family?

Part IV: Genesis 24:28-67

NT: Luke 19:11-28

Rebekah ran back to her house. She told her mother and the rest of her family all about Abraham's servant. When her brother Laban saw the jewelry, he went back to the well to find the man who had given his sister those things. Laban said, "Come, you who are blessed by YHVH! I have a room ready for you in my house."

Once they had unloaded the camels and sat down to dinner, Abraham's servant told Rebekah's family all about his orders to bring back a wife for Isaac. He told them that Abraham was a very wealthy man and that Isaac would inherit it all. Then he told them about his prayer by the well and how Rebekah had watered his camels.

Laban and Bethuel said, "YHVH is doing this." They told him that he could take Rebekah to Canaan and that she could become Isaac's wife. Rebekah agreed to go with him right away. Her family blessed her and sent her with Abraham's servant, and they sent her nurse with her.

When Abraham's servant arrived back at home, Isaac saw the camels coming. He saw Rebekah, and Rebekah looked up and saw him. Rebekah said, "Who is the man who is coming to meet us?" The servant told her that he was Isaac, and Rebekah covered herself with a veil. The servant told Isaac about everything that had happened, and Isaac married Rebekah right away. He loved her very much.

Discussion:

What did Rebekah's family think of what Abraham's servant told them?

What happened when Rebekah arrived back in Canaan?

What kind of person do you think Rebekah was?

Part V: Genesis 25:1-18

NT: Romans 9: 1-9

Abraham married a woman named Keturah. Keturah and Abraham were the parents of Zimran, Jokshan, Medan, Midian, Ishbak and Shuah. When Abraham's sons were old enough to leave home, he gave them gifts and sent them away from Isaac. Isaac was the only son who would inherit Abraham's possessions.

Abraham died when he was one hundred and seventy-five years old. Isaac and Ishmael buried their father in the cave where Sarah was buried. God blessed Isaac after Abraham died.

Ishmael had twelve sons, and they each became a leader of their own tribe. They lived on the eastern side of Egypt, and they fought with every tribe that was related to them.

Discussion:

Who was there to bury Abraham? Where was he buried?

How many sons did Ishmael have?

Toldot (History) –
Genesis 25:19 - 28:9; Malachi 1:1 - 2:7

Portion:

Part I: Genesis 25:19-34

NT: Hebrews 12:16; Acts 13:42-46

Abraham was the father of Isaac. Isaac married Rebekah when he was forty years old. For twenty years the couple waited for children, but Rebekah was not able to get pregnant. Isaac prayed to YHVH and asked Him to heal his wife. God healed Rebekah, and she became pregnant with twins.

From the very beginning, these twin brothers did not get along. They fought inside Rebekah's belly. When she asked God what was going on, He answered her and said, "These babies are two nations that will be separated from one another. The older brother will become the weaker nation, and he will serve the younger brother."

When it was time for the twins to be born, the first-born baby was red and hairy. They named him Esau, which means "hairy." As soon as Esau was born, there was the second baby –

holding on to Esau's foot. They named the second baby Jacob. Jacob means, "He grabs the heel."

The boys grew up, and Esau became a great hunter. He loved taking long hunting trips and living in the open land. Jacob was just the opposite; he liked to stay near home. Their father, Isaac, enjoyed eating the meat that Esau hunted, and Rebekah appreciated that Jacob stayed close to their home. Isaac loved Esau more than he loved Jacob, and Rebekah loved Jacob more than she loved Esau.

One day Esau came home hungry, and Jacob was in the kitchen making stew. Esau asked Jacob for some, and Jacob answered, "Sure! I'll trade you your inheritance for a bowl of stew." Esau was hungry and he agreed to this trade, so Jacob served Esau a meal. As the first-born, Esau should have received a double inheritance, but he traded his rights for one meal.

Discussion:

How long did Isaac and Rebekah wait for children?

What was unusual about Rebekah's pregnancy?

What does Jacob mean?

Why did Isaac like Esau more than Jacob?

Why did Esau sell his inheritance (birthright)?

Part II: Genesis 26:1-22

NT: Romans 12:9-21

Just like there had been in Abraham's time, another famine came to the land of Canaan. So, Isaac went to Gerar, to Abimelek the king of the Philistines. YHVH warned Isaac not to go to Egypt; He told him to stay in the land. Isaac obeyed God, and he stayed in Gerar. The men of Gerar asked Isaac about Rebekah, and he told them that Rebekah was his sister. She was very beautiful, and he was afraid they would kill him to marry her.

After Isaac and Rebekah had been in Gerar for a long time, Abimelek looked down from his window and saw the couple together. He could tell by the way they were acting that they were *not* brother and sister. He knew that he'd been lied to.

Abimelek called Isaac to him and said, "Why have you played this horrible trick? One of the men might have married your wife, and then we would all be cursed!"

Isaac explained that he had been afraid. Abimelek told all his people that they were not allowed to hurt Rebekah or Isaac.

Isaac planted crops in Gerar, and YHVH blessed his harvest one hundred times more than what he had planted. Isaac became a very rich man. Because he was so wealthy, the Philistines were jealous of him. They began to ruin Abraham's wells by filling them back with dirt.

Abimelek said to Isaac, "You have become too powerful; you need to move away." Isaac listened and moved away to the Valley of Gerar. Isaac re-dug the wells that had belonged to Abraham, and he gave them the same names that his father had given them.

Then Isaac's servants dug a new well, but the shepherds who lived in the valley fought with Isaac over it. They said, "The water is ours!" Isaac named the well *Esek*, because that means "argument." Then Isaac's servants dug another well, but the shepherds wanted that one, too. Isaac named that well *Sitnah* or "opposition." Again, Isaac moved a little way away, and his servants dug another well. No one fought with them for this well. Isaac named the well *Rehoboth*, because Rehoboth means "room." God had given Isaac and his household room to live well in the land.

Discussion:

Why did Isaac lie and say that Rebekah was his sister?

Why did Abimelek want Isaac to move away?

How did Isaac know he had found a good place to live?

Part III: Genesis 26:23-33

NT: I Corinthians 11:23-34

After a while, Isaac moved to Beersheba. YHVH came to Isaac and said, "I am the God of your father, Abraham. Don't be afraid! I am with you! I will bless you and give you many descendants because of My promise to Abraham."

Isaac built an altar to YHVH, and he settled in Beersheba. His servants began to dig a well.

Abimelek left Gerar and went to Beersheba to find Isaac. He brought some important men with him. When Isaac saw the men, he said, "Why have you come all the way to find me after you were so rude in sending me away?"

Abimelek said, "We can see that YHVH is with you, and we want to make an agreement with you. Remember that we did not harm you, and now you are blessed. We want *you* to promise that you will not harm us now."

Isaac agreed, and then he served a big meal. The men all ate and drank together. They promised not to harm one another. After feasting, Abimelek and his men went back toward Gerar.

That same day, Isaac's servants came to him with news about the well they were digging. "We have found water!" they said. Isaac named the well *Shibah,* which means "oath" or "promise."

Discussion:

Who came to Isaac to make a peace agreement with him? Why?

Why did Isaac serve them a meal?

Part IV: Genesis 26:34-27:40

NT: Hebrews 11:20

When Esau was forty years old, he married two Hittite women. They made life very difficult for Isaac and Rebekah.

Isaac was old, and he had gone blind. He didn't know how much longer he would live, so he felt it was time to bless his firstborn son.

Isaac called to Esau and said, "Go into the country and hunt some meat. Prepare it the way I like it, and bring it to me. I am going to give you your blessing."

Once Esau had gone, Rebekah called to Jacob. She said, "Your father is ready to give Esau his blessing. Listen to me, and do exactly what I tell you to do."

Rebekah told Jacob to get a goat from their herd. She would cook it the way Isaac liked it, and then Jacob would pretend he was Esau.

Jacob was afraid to trick his father; he worried that Isaac would catch him and would curse him instead of blessing him. His mother said that she would take any curse for him; she covered Jacob's arms and hands with goatskin so that he would be hairy like Esau. She gave him Esau's clothes to wear, too.

Jacob pretended to be Esau, and he took a meal to his father. At first Isaac was suspicious, but Jacob told him, "I am Esau." Isaac couldn't see, and because Jacob smelled like Esau and was hairy like Esau, Isaac gave Jacob the blessing.

He said, "May YHVH give you rain and harvest. May you rule over nations. May anyone who curses you be cursed, and may anyone who blesses you be blessed."

Almost as soon as Jacob left his father, Esau came in with a meal. This was a shock to Isaac, and he was very upset. "I've already blessed your brother!" he said.

Esau cried, "Can't you bless me, too?"

Isaac told Esau that he would not be blessed. He said that he would serve his brother—just as YHVH told Rebekah when she was pregnant with the boys.

Discussion:

Who had Esau married? Did his parents like his wives?

Who decided to trick Isaac?

What did they do?

Part V: Genesis 27:41-28:9

NT: Galatians 6:7-9

Esau was very angry. He planned to kill Jacob as soon as their father died. When Rebekah heard this, she was worried. Rebekah called for Jacob. She said, "Go to my hometown, and live with my brother, Laban. Don't come back until Esau has forgotten about what you did. I will let you know when it is safe."

Then Rebekah spoke to her husband and said, "Isaac, I am miserable living with Esau's wives! I'd rather die than see Jacob married to a woman from Canaan, too!"

Isaac blessed Jacob and sent him to Rebekah's hometown. He told him not to marry a Canaanite woman but instead to marry one of his Uncle Laban's daughters.

When Esau heard this, he realized how upset he had made his parents by marrying Canaanite women. Then Esau married a third woman: a daughter of Ishmael.

Discussion:

Why did Rebekah want Jacob to go away?

What did Rebekah tell Isaac?

When Esau heard that his parents were upset by his wives, what did he do?

Vayetze (He went out) – Genesis 28:10 - 32:2; Hosea 11:7 - 14:10

Portion:

Part I: Genesis 28:10-22

NT: Matthew 23:16-22; John 1:43-51

Jacob left Beersheba and headed for Harran. He stopped to camp for the night, and he used a rock for a pillow. While he was sleeping, he had an amazing dream. Jacob saw a stairway that reached from heaven down to the earth, and he saw angels walking up and down it. YHVH stood beside him, and He spoke to Jacob. He said, "Jacob, I am YHVH. I am the God of Abraham and Isaac. I will give you and your people the land you are sleeping on now. You will have so many descendants that they will be like the dust covering the earth. All the people of the earth will be blessed because of your family. I will be with you, and I will protect you, and I will bring you back to this land."

Jacob knew his dream was special. He knew it was more than a dream. He said, "Surely YHVH is here, and I didn't even know it! This is the house of God and the door to heaven!"

The next morning, Jacob took the rock he had slept on and set it up as a reminder. He poured oil on the rock, and he called the place "Bethel," because Bethel means "House of God."

Jacob made a promise to God. He said, "God, if You really will be with me and protect me—if You will feed me and clothe me and bring me safely back home—then You will be my God, and I will serve You here. I will give You back ten percent of everything You give me."

Discussion:

What did Jacob see and hear in his dream?

What does Bethel mean?

Part II: Genesis 29:1-30

NT: John 4:1-29; Galatians 6:7-10

When Jacob had reached his destination, he came to a well of water surrounded by open land. Sheep were resting near the well, and the well was covered by a very large stone. The local shepherds would meet at the well. When they were all there, the shepherds would work together to move the stone and water their animals. After they were finished, the shepherds would work together to put the stone back in its place.

Jacob walked up to the shepherds and asked them," My brothers, where are you from?"

They answered and said, "We're from Harran."

Jacob asked them if they knew his uncle Laban, and the shepherds told him that they did. They said, "Here comes Laban's daughter with his sheep, now!"

When Jacob saw Rachel coming, he said to the shepherds who were with him, "Water your sheep, and take them back to the field to eat." But they would not, because the other shepherds had not come yet.

When Rachel arrived with Laban's sheep, Jacob went over to the well. He moved the stone by himself, and he watered his uncle Laban's sheep. Jacob was so overwhelmed with joy that he kissed Rachel and cried out loud. He told her that he was her Aunt Rebekah's son. When Rachel heard this, she ran to tell her father.

Laban ran to meet Jacob. Laban welcomed Jacob into his home and as a part of his family.

Jacob lived with Laban, and he worked for him as a shepherd. After he had been there a month, Laban said, "It's not right for you to work for free just because you're family. What should I pay you?"

Laban had two daughters. Leah was older, but Jacob was in love with Laban's younger daughter, Rachel. Jacob said, "I will work seven years if you will allow me to marry Rachel." Laban liked this idea, and so Jacob stayed and worked. The years flew by because Jacob loved Rachel so much.

When the seven years were over, Jacob said to Laban, "I have worked seven years; give me my wife."

Laban held a wedding feast for all of their friends and neighbors. After the feasting, Laban took his older daughter, Leah, and he sent her into Jacob's tent instead of Rachel. Jacob was tricked into marrying Leah.

When the sun rose the next morning, Jacob saw that he'd married Leah instead of Rachel. His heart was broken! He ran to Laban and said, "I served you for Rachel, didn't I? Why have you tricked me?"

Laban told Jacob that it was their tradition for the oldest daughter to marry first. He said, "Finish a one-week honeymoon with Leah; then you may marry Rachel, too. After you have married Rachel, you'll work seven more years to pay the bride-price for *her*."

So, Jacob married both of Laban's daughters. As a wedding present, Laban gave both of his daughters a female servant to help her in her new home. Leah's servant's name was Zilpah, and Rachel's servant's name was Bilhah.

Jacob loved Rachel more than he loved Leah. He worked another seven years for Rachel.

Discussion:

Where was the first place Jacob went when he arrived in Laban's town?

Why do you think Jacob wanted the other shepherds to hurry and leave the well?

What did Jacob do when Rachel arrived at the well?

What did Rachel's father think of Jacob?

What did Jacob want as payment for working for Laban?

How long did he agree to work as payment for Rachel?

At the end of the seven years, what did Laban do?

Part III: Genesis 29:31-30:24

NT: I John 5:14-15

The Lord saw that Leah was not loved, and he had mercy on her. He allowed Leah to have children while her loved sister, Rachel, could not. Leah became pregnant with a son. She named him **Reuben**, because Reuben means, "God has seen my misery." Leah had a second son, and she named him **Simeon**. Simeon means, "One who hears." Leah named her third son **Levi** which means "attached." She hoped that by having his sons, Jacob would become attached to her. Then Leah had a fourth son, and she named him **Judah**, meaning "praise." After Judah, Leah didn't have any more children for a while.

Now Leah had four sons, and Rachel did not have any. Rachel was very jealous of her sister. She went to Jacob and said, "Give me children! I cannot live like this!" This made Jacob angry. He said, "Am I the one keeping you from having children—or is it God?"

Then Rachel told Jacob to have children with her servant, Bilhah. "They will be my children, because she is my servant," she said.

Jacob had a son with Rachel's servant, Bilhah, and Rachel named the baby **Dan**. Dan means "vindicated" or "proven innocent." Rachel felt vindicated by God because she had given Jacob a son through her servant. Then Bilhah had another son, and Rachel named him **Naphtali**. Naphtali means "my struggle."

Leah hadn't had any more children, so she also gave her servant to Jacob and asked him to have children with her. Leah's servant, Zilpah, had a son. Leah named him **Gad** because Gad means "What good fortune!" Then Leah's servant had another son. Leah named him **Asher** because Asher means "happy."

Leah became pregnant again. She had a fifth son named **Issachar**, meaning "reward," and then a sixth son named **Zebulun**, meaning "honor." After a little while, Leah also had a daughter. She named her Dinah.

Then God had mercy on Rachel and allowed her to become pregnant. Rachel had a son, and she named him **Joseph**. Joseph means, "May He add another son."

Discussion:

Why did Rachel name Bilhah's baby "Dan"? Why did she need to be proven innocent?

Why did God allow Leah to have children before Rachel?

How many sons of Jacob can you name?

Part IV: Genesis 30:25-43

NT: Matthew 10

After Joseph was born, Jacob was ready to return to his own land: the land that God had promised him. Jacob went to Laban and told him he was ready to leave. "I have worked hard for you," he said. "Give me my wives and children. It's time to let me go."

This worried Laban. Through fortune-telling, Laban learned that he was blessed because of Jacob. "Please stay with me," Laban said. "I'll pay you whatever you want."

Jacob asked Laban to give him all the spotted or speckled lambs and goats and all the black sheep. These animals would be his payment. He would continue to work for Laban, and Laban would keep the rest of the flock. Laban told Jacob that he agreed.

Then Laban went through his flock and took all the black sheep and every sheep or goat that was speckled, spotted, or streaked. He gave them to his sons to watch over. He traveled three-day's distance from Jacob so that Jacob could not use these animals for breeding a new speckled or spotted flock.

Jacob had an idea. He stripped the bark from tree branches so that the branches were striped: dark bark and light wood. He put these striped branches into the flock's water. The flock would drink from the water, and then their babies would be speckled and spotted. Jacob took these new spotted and speckled animals, and he separated them from Laban's solid-colored animals. If the animals that came to drink water were weak, Jacob removed the striped sticks. If the animals that came to drink were strong, he placed the striped sticks in the water. This is how Jacob made a stronger, larger flock for himself and a weaker, smaller flock for Laban. Jacob became very rich.

Discussion:

What did Jacob ask Laban to let him keep as his payment for shepherding Laban's flock?

What did Laban do after agreeing to this deal?

What happened to Jacob's flock? Laban's flock?

Part V: Genesis 31:1-32:2

NT: James 1

Jacob heard that Laban's sons were complaining about his success and accusing him of stealing. He also noticed that Laban was not quite as nice to him as he had been. Jacob knew it was time to go home, so he called his wives to the field and told them about a dream God had given him. In the dream, God had promised Jacob all the spotted and speckled animals. God had kept His word. In the dream, God had also reminded Jacob of the promise He made to Him at Bethel, and God had told Jacob to go back home.

Rachel and Leah knew that their father had cheated their husband. They told Jacob to obey what God said. Jacob put his wives and children on camels, and they left with all their livestock and things. Before they left, Rachel stole her father's idols. Jacob did not know that she took them.

Three days after Jacob and his family left in secret, Laban found out that they had gone. He went after them, and he caught up with them seven days later. Laban said, "Why did you run away? I would have thrown you a goodbye party. And why did you have to take my gods?" Laban said.

Jacob answered, "I was afraid you would try to stop us from going, but we did not take your gods. If anyone has taken your gods, that person will die."

Laban looked for the idols, but he could not find them because Rachel was sitting on them.

Jacob told Laban, "I have worked for you for twenty years of long hours in bad weather. I have served you faithfully, and you have cheated me over and over again. The only reason I am wealthy is because God has blessed me. God has seen how you have treated me."

Laban said, "Everything you have is *mine*. Still, let's make a promise to never harm each other. Promise to be good to my daughters, and do not marry any women but them."

Jacob set up stones as a witness of his promise, and he made an agreement with Laban. They all feasted together, and the next morning Laban returned home.

Jacob went toward Canaan, and God sent His messengers to meet him. When Jacob saw the messengers, he said, "This is the camp of God!"

Discussion:

What did Jacob tell his wives about the dream God had given him?

What did Rachel steal before they left?

Jacob knew God had blessed him and made him wealthy. Did Laban agree?

What did Jacob and Laban promise each other?

Vayishlach (He sent) –
Genesis 32:3 - 36:43; Hosea 11:7 - 12:12; Obadiah 1:1-21

Portion:

Part I: Genesis 32:3-32

NT: Matthew 6:5-8; Luke 1:67-80

Jacob sent servants ahead of him with a message for his brother, Esau. They said, "Your servant Jacob has been with Laban all these years, and he has become a wealthy man. He hopes you will welcome him home." When Esau heard their message, he got ready to meet Jacob. He took four hundred men with him on the trip.

When his servants told Jacob that his brother was coming with four hundred men, Jacob was very afraid. Jacob divided his people and animals into two separate groups. He hoped that if Esau came and attacked one camp, the other camp would be able to escape.

Jacob prayed to YHVH. He thanked God for blessing him so much. He had left Canaan with nothing, and now he had enough for two camps. He reminded God of His promises to him: promises to make him a very large nation. Then Jacob sent gifts to Esau.

Jacob sent one servant with a herd of sheep and another servant with a herd of goats. He sent a servant with a herd of camels, a servant with a herd of cows, and a servant with a herd of donkeys. He did not send them together because he wanted each servant to present a separate gift. Jacob hoped that with each gift Esau would become a little less angry and would change his mind about wanting to kill him.

After he'd sent his servants with the gifts, Jacob stayed in the camp. But in the middle of the night, he got up. He sent his wives and children across a stream with everything he owned. Then, when Jacob was completely alone, a man came and wrestled him to the ground. They wrestled all night long. Jacob would not let go of the man—even when the man grabbed his hip and pulled it from its socket. When the sun was almost up, the man said to Jacob, "Let me go!" Jacob answered, "I won't let You go until You bless me!" Jacob knew he was wrestling with God.

There God changed Jacob's name to Israel because Israel means "struggles with God." Jacob called the place Peniel. Peniel means "face of God." Through the dim, early light of sunrise, Jacob had seen God's face, and he had been allowed to live.

Discussion:

Think back: Why was Jacob afraid of Esau?

What did Esau do when he received the message from Jacob's servants?

Think back: What does Jacob mean?

What does Israel mean?

What is the difference between grabbing a heel and struggling with God?

Why was Jacob wrestling with God?

Part II: Genesis 33:1-20

NT: Luke 6:36-38

When Jacob looked up, he saw Esau coming with four hundred men. Jacob was still afraid, so he separated his children and their mothers into groups. He sent the servants with their children first, Leah and her children next, and he hid Rachel and Joseph in the back. Then Jacob walked toward Esau and his men—bowing seven times before he got there. But Esau did not try to hurt Jacob; he ran to meet him instead. He hugged him and kissed him, and they cried together because they had missed each other so much.

"Who is with you?" Esau asked. Then Jacob introduced his children and their mothers to Esau.

"Why did I pass so many herds of animals?" Esau asked.

"Those are gifts from me to you. I wanted to make you happy with me," Jacob said.

Esau answered, "Oh, no, I already have plenty!" But Jacob talked Esau into accepting his gifts.

Esau asked Jacob to travel with him to his home, but Jacob told him that the young animals and children were too tired to go any farther that day. Jacob told Esau that he would meet him later. So, Esau headed toward *his* home, and Jacob went to Sukkoth and made shelters for himself and his animals.

When Jacob arrived in Canaan, he camped outside the city of Shechem on a piece of land that he bought for one hundred pieces of silver. Jacob set up an altar to God, and he called the place *El Elohe Israel*, which means "Mighty is the God of Israel."

Discussion:

Did Esau come to kill Jacob?

Why do you think Esau brought 400 men?

Why did Jacob put Rachel and Joseph in back?

Part III: Genesis 34:1-31

NT: Romans 12:17-20

[Mature content ahead.]

One day, while Jacob and his family were living near the city, Leah's daughter, Dinah, went out to meet the women who lived in the land. The prince of the land was named Shechem. When Shechem saw Dinah, he wanted her for himself. So Shechem took Dinah, and he slept with her as only husbands and wives should. After this happened, Shechem spoke sincerely and lovingly to Dinah. He felt love for her, and he wanted to marry her. Shechem asked his father to speak with Dinah's family to arrange their marriage and plan their wedding. So Hamor, the ruler of the land, went to speak with Jacob. Shechem told Dinah's brothers that they could set the bride price as high as they wanted. He was willing to pay any amount.

When Dinah's brothers heard about this crime that had been committed against Israel and their sister, they were very angry. They lied to Shechem, and they told him that they would arrange his marriage as soon as he and his men were circumcised. "We cannot give our sister to an uncircumcised man," they said.

Immediately, Hamor and Shechem were circumcised (and so were all the men in their city). While they were still recovering and in pain, Simeon and Levi (sons of Leah) went into the city and killed every man with a sword. They took Dinah from Shechem's house, and they took all the riches of the city along with the women and children.

When Jacob saw what they had done, he was very angry. His sons had put his family at risk by making them a threat to the people who lived around them. Jacob worried that the people of the land would gang up on them and defeat them.

Discussion:

Do you think that Shechem was repentant?

Was circumcision a small price to pay?

Would it be right for a daughter of Jacob to marry an uncircumcised man?

What do you think of what Levi and Simeon did?

Part IV: Genesis 35:1-29

NT: James 4:7-9

God told Jacob to go back to the place where he'd seen the staircase reaching to heaven: the place Jacob had called Bethel. Jacob called for his wives and children and everyone traveling with him. He told them to get rid of the foreign gods they were carrying, and Jacob buried the idols under a tree at Shechem. He told them to take a bath and to change their clothes. They were going to Bethel: the house of God. No one chased Jacob to attack his family because God had made the people afraid of them.

While they were camped at Bethel, God appeared to Jacob again. Again, God told him that his new name was Israel. He would not be called Jacob anymore. God also reminded him of His promises. He said, "I will give you and your descendants the land I promised to Abraham and Isaac; I will make you a nation and a group of nations. Kings will come from you." Jacob built an altar to God.

Rebekah's nurse, Deborah, had died and was buried under an oak tree outside Bethel. That place was named *Allon Bakuth*, which means "oak of weeping."

After they left Bethel, and before they reached the next town, Rachel went into labor. She was pregnant with her second son. She had a very difficult labor, and she died right after the baby was born. Rachel named him "son of my trouble," but Jacob changed the baby's name to *Benjamin*, meaning "son of my right hand."

[Mature content ahead.]

Israel moved again. While they were camped past Migdal Eder, Reuben slept with Bilhah, the servant that Rachel had given to Jacob. Jacob found out about it.

Jacob moved to Hebron where Abraham had lived. Isaac was still alive, and he lived to be one hundred and eighty years old. Esau and Jacob were both there when it was time to bury their father.

Discussion:

Why did God tell Jacob to go back to Bethel?

Why did Jacob instruct his family to wash, change, and get rid of the "gods"?

What did God tell Jacob at Bethel?

What does Benjamin mean?

Who buried Isaac?

Part V: Genesis 36:1-43

NT: Hebrews 12:3-17

Esau's three wives gave him five sons: Eliphaz, Reuel, Jeush, Jalam and Korah. Both Jacob and Esau were wealthy men, and the land was too crowded for them to continue living near one another. Esau packed up and moved away from Jacob to the hill country of Seir (that is called Edom). Esau's descendants were the Edomites, and they ruled the land of Edom before any Israelite king ruled.

Discussion:

Why did Esau move away from Jacob?

Vayeshev (He continued living) – Genesis 37:1 - 40:23; Amos 2:6 - 3:8

Portion:

Part I: Genesis 37:1-11

NT: Luke 2:41-52

Jacob, now called Israel, stayed in the land of Canaan and raised his family there. When his son Joseph was seventeen years old, he came home from the field where he had been caring for the sheep with his brothers. Joseph was not happy about the way his brothers were acting, and he told his father about it. Joseph, the eleventh son, was Israel's favorite. Israel gave Joseph a long robe to show how much he loved him. This made his brothers hate him.

Joseph had a dream that he and his brothers were all in the field tying stalks of grain. In the dream, Joseph's grain stood up tall while his brothers' sheaves gathered around it and bowed down to it. Joseph told his brothers about his dream, and then they hated him more.

Joseph had another dream where the sun, moon, and eleven stars all bowed to him. His father corrected Joseph for having a dream like that. Still, Israel couldn't stop wondering about it.

Discussion:

How many older brothers did Joseph have?

What did Joseph's brothers think of him?

Can you think of a reason why Joseph's brothers didn't like him?

Part II: Genesis 37:12-36

NT: Matthew 26:1-27:3

Joseph's brothers were near Shechem with their father's flocks, and Israel wondered how they were doing. He knew Joseph would tell him if there was any trouble, so he sent Joseph to check on them. When Joseph got there, he couldn't find his brothers anywhere. They were not where they were supposed to be. Joseph asked a man who he saw in the field, and the man told him where they had gone.

Joseph went to find his brothers, and his brothers saw

Joseph coming. They were angry, and they wanted to kill him. Reuben talked them into throwing Joseph into an old, empty well instead. He planned to go back to rescue him later.

With Joseph at the bottom of the well, his brothers sat down and ate lunch. While they were eating, a large group of Ishmaelites (also called Midianites) came traveling by. They had spices and medicines, and they were headed to Egypt to sell them.

Judah had an idea. "Let's sell Joseph to these Ishmaelites!" he said. "After all, we shouldn't kill our own brother." Reuben was not there at the time, and the rest of the brothers agreed: They sold Joseph to the Ishmaelites for twenty shekels of silver.

When Reuben got back to the well to get his brother, he saw that Joseph was not there. He tore his clothes and cried, "What will I do now?" Then Reuben helped his brothers to cover up their crime. They killed a goat and soaked Joseph's beautiful robe with blood. Then they took the robe to their father. Israel recognized the robe, and he was sure that Joseph had been killed by a wild animal while on his way to find his brothers.

Israel was extremely upset, and no one in his whole family could comfort him. He didn't know that at just that moment

Joseph was alive and being sold to a man named Potiphar: captain of the army in Egypt.

Discussion:

When Joseph went looking for his brothers, were they where his father said they would be?

What did Joseph's brothers do when they saw him coming?

Where did Joseph's brothers put him?

How did Joseph's brothers convince Israel/Jacob that Joseph was dead?

Part III: Genesis 38:1-30

NT: Matthew 1:1-6

[Mature content ahead.]

Judah left home and married a Canaanite woman. They had three sons. When Judah's oldest son, Er, was old enough to marry, Judah found a wife for him. Her name was Tamar. Er was a wicked man, and God killed Er before he and Tamar had any children.

Judah had a second son named Onan. Judah told him,

"Marry Tamar and give her children for your brother." But Onan refused to give Tamar children, so God killed Onan, too.

Judah's third son, Shelah, was young. Judah was afraid that if Shelah married Tamar he would die as well. So, Judah said to Tamar, "Go back to your father's house, and wait until Shelah is old enough for marriage." Tamar obeyed.

Many years later, long after Shelah was grown, Judah's wife died. Tamar saw that she was never going to be married to Shelah. She knew that the only way she could have children from her husband's family would be to have a child with Judah. Tamar disguised herself as a prostitute, and she tricked her lonely father-in-law.

Tamar had a plan. Before she would sleep with Judah, she asked him what he would pay her. He told her that he'd give her a young goat. Tamar asked to hold Judah's seal, cord, and staff until he returned with the goat. Judah agreed, and he gave Tamar the items she asked for.

After Judah left, Tamar took off her disguise and changed back into her regular clothes. Judah sent a man with the goat as payment, but Tamar was nowhere to be found.

A little while later, Judah heard that Tamar was pregnant and without a husband. Judah demanded that she be killed. Just as Tamar was being brought before the crowd, she had a message delivered to Judah along with the things he had given her. The note said, "I am pregnant by the man who owns *these* things." Judah was shocked. He said, "She is more righteous than I am! I should have given her to my son, Shelah!"

Tamar gave birth to twin boys. The babies fought over who would be born first. When the first baby reached out his arm, the midwife tied a red string around his wrist. Then that baby pulled his arm back, and his brother was born first. They named the baby who was born first *Perez*, because Perez means "breaking out." They named the second baby *Zerah* because of the red thread around his arm. Zerah means "bright red."

Discussion:

The Law demanded that a brother marry his brother's widow if her husband had not given her children. How did Onan and Judah break this law?

The items Tamar asked Judah to give her were his identification—like a wallet and I.D. card are today. Why did she do this?

Why did Judah say that Tamar was more right (righteous) than he was?

Part IV: Genesis 39:1-23

NT: II Timothy 2:20-26

[Mature content ahead.]

Remember Joseph? He'd been sold to a man named Potiphar. YHVH was with Joseph in everything that Joseph did, and so He blessed Potiphar because of Joseph. Potiphar saw that everything Joseph did was greatly blessed, and Potiphar put Joseph in charge of everything that he owned.

Joseph was handsome, and Potiphar's wife was not a faithful woman. She wanted to be with Joseph. Day after day she kept asking and asking, but Joseph always told her no. One day Joseph ran from Potiphar's wife, and she grabbed his coat as he ran. She was angry at Joseph for rejecting her. She took Joseph's torn coat to her husband, and she told him a lie about Joseph. She told her husband that Joseph had attacked her and that he had run away when she screamed. Potiphar believed his wife, and he locked Joseph in the king's prison.

Even in prison, YHVH blessed Joseph, and the prison warden put Joseph in charge of everything that happened in the prison.

Discussion:

What did Potiphar think of Joseph?

What did the warden of the prison think of Joseph?

Was Joseph put into prison for doing something wrong?

Was Joseph put into prison for doing something right?

Part V: Genesis 40:1-23

NT: I Peter 3:15-17

After Joseph had been in prison a while, the king's baker and cupbearer did things that upset the king. Pharaoh sent them to prison, and Joseph was in charge of them.

One night, both the cupbearer and the baker had dreams that worried them. Joseph said, "Dreams and their meanings are from God. Tell me your dreams."

The cupbearer said that he dreamed of a grape vine with three branches. It budded and blossomed and ripened into grapes. In his dream, he squeezed the grapes into Pharaoh's cup and then handed it straight to him.

Joseph interpreted the dream. He told the cupbearer that in three days he would be released from prison. He would go back to work serving wine to the king.

The cupbearer was thrilled with the interpretation, and Joseph said, "Please, when you're back with the king, tell him about me. Tell him that I've done nothing wrong."

When the baker saw that the cupbearer's dream was a happy one, he told his dream to Joseph, too. In the baker's dream, he carried three baskets of bread on his head. The bread was for Pharaoh, but the birds were eating it.

Joseph interpreted the baker's dream, too. He told him that after three days he would be put to death.

Three days later, it was the Pharaoh's birthday. He made the decision to give the cupbearer back his job, and he executed the baker—just as Joseph had said. The cupbearer was back with the king, but he forgot to tell the king about Joseph.

Discussion:

What did the cupbearer and the baker's dreams have in common?

Miketz (At the end) –
Genesis 41:1 - 44:17; I Kings 3:15 - 4:1; Zech. 2:14 - 4:7

Portion:

Part I: Genesis 41:1-40

NT: Matthew 2:10-20

Two years after Pharaoh's cupbearer was released from prison, Joseph was still there. Then Pharaoh had a nightmare, and none of his usual advisors were able to interpret it for him. This reminded the cupbearer of Joseph, and he felt sorry for forgetting about him. The cupbearer told Pharaoh about Joseph and how he had interpreted his dream.

Pharaoh sent for Joseph immediately. Joseph shaved and changed, and he went to Pharaoh. Pharaoh told Joseph his dream. Pharaoh said, "I was standing on the edge of the Nile River. Up out of the water walked seven fat and healthy cows, and they ate the tall grass along the river. Then seven skinny and sickly cows came out of the river. The skinny cows ate the fat cows. After they ate them, the skinny cows were just as skinny as before! That's when I woke up. When I went back to sleep, I had another dream. I saw seven good heads of grain all growing on a single stalk of wheat. Then seven more heads of wheat sprouted, and they were withered by the wind and burned by the sun. The seven ruined heads of grain swallowed the seven good heads."

Joseph said to Pharaoh, "These two dreams are the same. God is showing you what He is about to do. The seven fat cows and the seven healthy heads of wheat are seven years of good harvest; there will be more than enough to eat in those years. The seven skinny cows and the seven ruined heads of wheat are the seven years of famine that will come after the good years; there will be nothing to eat in those years. God has shown you this twice because He will not change His mind. This is what will happen."

Joseph advised Pharaoh and said, "You need to find a wise man you can trust. Put him in charge of storing up grain during the seven years when too much grows. Save one-fifth of the grain from those years. Then, when the famine comes, all of Egypt will have enough to buy and eat!"

Pharaoh saw that Joseph was wise and that God had given him a plan. He said, "I will put you in charge! In all of Egypt, second only to me, no one will be more powerful than you!"

Discussion:

How long did Joseph remain in prison after the cupbearer was released?

Why was Joseph released from prison?

What did Pharaoh dream?

What did Pharaoh's dreams mean?

Do you think it was God's plan for Joseph to stay in prison until Pharaoh needed him?

Part II: Genesis 41:41-57

NT: Matthew 25:14-30

Pharaoh put Joseph in charge of Egypt—second only to himself. He gave Joseph his ring as well as royal clothing and jewelry. Pharaoh made sure that everyone in Egypt knew that Joseph was in charge. Pharaoh gave Joseph a wife; she was the daughter of the priest of the sun god. Joseph was given the Egyptian name Zaphnath-Paaneah. His wife's name was Asenath. All of this happened when Joseph was thirty years old.

Joseph gathered and stored grain during the first seven years; there was so much to gather that after a while he stopped weighing and measuring it. There was plenty to eat, and there was plenty to save for the famine. During these seven years, Joseph and his wife had two sons. The first son's name was *Manasseh*, meaning "forget," because Joseph had forgotten his troubles. His second son's name was *Ephraim*, meaning "twice fruitful."

When the seven years of plenty were over, the years of famine began. When the people were hungry, Pharaoh sent them to Joseph to buy grain. All over the lands surrounding Egypt, there was famine. Only in Egypt was there food to eat.

Discussion:

What was Joseph's job in Egypt?

Who did Joseph marry?

What were the names of Joseph's sons?

Part III: Genesis 42:1-28

NT: I Peter 3:8-12

When Joseph's father, Israel, heard that there was grain in Egypt, he told his ten oldest sons to go and buy some. He kept Benjamin at home with him because he was afraid something might happen to him if he went along.

Joseph was the one in charge of selling grain. His brothers didn't recognize him, and they came and bowed low before him. Joseph pretended he didn't recognize them either, but he did. When his brothers bowed to him, Joseph remembered the dreams he had before being sold into slavery.

When they told Joseph they had come from Canaan to buy grain, Joseph said, "Liars! You are spies! You have come to see the horrible famine of the land and to see how weak Egypt has become!"

"No!" They answered, "We are twelve brothers: sons of one man in Canaan. Our youngest brother is at home with our father, and one brother is no longer living."

"Fine," Joseph answered. "Prove it. You won't leave here until your youngest brother comes to join you. One of you may leave and bring him back." Then Joseph put his brothers in prison. After three days, Joseph said, "Just one of you will stay here in prison; the rest of you will go and bring back your brother. If you have a younger brother, I will know you were telling the truth. Then you will not die."

Joseph's brothers talked together. They knew they were being punished for selling Joseph into slavery, but they still did not realize they were standing in front of him now. Joseph used an interpreter when he spoke to his brothers. They didn't know he spoke their language, but Joseph knew what they were saying. He left the room to cry.

When Joseph came back into the room, he ordered the guards to tie Simeon's hands and feet. He commanded his men saying, "Fill the Canaanites' bags with the grain they came to buy, but also put their money back in their bags." Joseph's brothers did not know what he was saying.

Joseph locked Simeon in prison. The rest of the brothers loaded up their donkeys with the grain they'd bought, and they headed back to Canaan. When they stopped along the way to feed their donkeys, one of the brothers opened his sack of grain. When he found the money he'd used to pay for the grain, he was very afraid. They were already in trouble with the ruler in Egypt, and now it looked like they were thieves! "What is God doing to us?" they asked.

Discussion:

Why didn't Joseph's brothers recognize him?

Was Joseph nice to his brothers?

What did Joseph accuse his brothers of being?

How could they prove that they were not spies?

Part IV: Genesis 42:29-43:14

NT: James 5:12

When the nine brothers arrived home without Simeon, they told their father about everything that had happened. Then they each opened their sacks of grain and discovered that *everyone's* money was there. They were all afraid!

Israel said, "This is a terrible thing! Joseph is gone, now Simeon is gone, and you want to take Benjamin, too? No! You will not take him!"

Reuben said, "Let my two sons die if anything happens to Benjamin!" Israel would not let him go, so they didn't return to

Egypt right away. However, when they'd eaten all of the grain they'd brought back from Egypt, Israel wanted them to go and buy more. Judah said, "Father, the man in Egypt warned us. We *cannot* return without Benjamin. Let Benjamin go with us, and I promise to bring him back safely. Let the blame be on me forever if anything happens to him. If we don't go back for grain, *all* of us will die!"

Finally, Israel let Benjamin go. He sent his sons with double the price of grain so they could return the money that had been put in their sacks. He also sent them with a gift for the man in Egypt: a little of all the best things in Canaan.

Discussion:

Did Israel want them to take Benjamin to Egypt? Why?

Why did he let him go?

Part V: Genesis 43:15-44:17

NT: II Corinthians 7; Acts 11:1-18

When Joseph saw that his brothers had returned with Benjamin, he ordered his servant to kill an animal and to prepare a big feast in his home. The servant told Joseph's brothers that they would be eating with his master. The brothers asked the servant about the money that had been returned to their sacks. "We don't know who put it there, but we've brought it all back," they said. The servant answered, "Don't be afraid. It wasn't a mistake." Then he returned Simeon to them.

All of Joseph's brothers waited for him in his home. They prepared the gifts they had brought for him. When Joseph arrived, they bowed before him. Joseph asked them about their father. Then Joseph saw Benjamin, and he wanted to cry. He said, "Is this your younger brother who you told me about?" Joseph blessed Benjamin; then he left the room to cry because he had missed Benjamin so much.

When Joseph came back to the room, his servants set the places for lunch. They set Joseph a place by himself, the brothers a place by themselves, and the Egyptian guests a place by themselves. Egyptians did not eat with Hebrews; that was disgusting to Egyptians. Joseph's brothers were seated from oldest to youngest. The brothers were amazed that the Egyptians knew their ages. Then the food was served, and Benjamin was served five times as much as the others.

Joseph said to his servant, "Send the men with as much grain as they can carry. Put their money back in their sacks, and put my silver cup at the top of Benjamin's sack." His servant obeyed. Early the next morning, Joseph sent his brothers back to Canaan.

When the brothers were just a little way from Egypt, Joseph sent his servant out after them. He told his servant to accuse the eleven brothers of stealing his silver cup.

When the brothers were accused, they said, "We brought back the money that had been put in our sacks! Are we the kind of men who would steal a cup? Search our bags! If you find the cup, the man who took it will die. The rest of us will be your slaves."

The brothers' sacks were searched—starting with the oldest brother's first. When they opened Benjamin's sack, there was the silver cup! The brothers were terrified! They mourned, and they tore their clothes. Then they headed back to Egypt for punishment.

When they arrived at Joseph's house, they threw themselves down at his feet. Judah said, "God has revealed our sin. There is nothing we can say to prove our innocence. We will all be your slaves, the rest of us and the one who had the cup in his sack."

But Joseph said, "I would never do such a terrible thing. Only the guilty man will be my slave. The rest of you may go."

Discussion:

What did Joseph do when he saw his brothers coming with Benjamin?

What happened at lunch that seemed strange to Joseph's brothers?

Why do you think Joseph put his cup in Benjamin's sack?

Why did Judah say that God had revealed their guilt? Was he talking about the theft of the silver cup?

Vayigash (He approached) –
Genesis 44:18 - 47:27; Ezekiel 37:15-28

Portion:

Part I: Genesis 44:18-34

NT: I John 3:16-24

Judah was very afraid. He still had no idea that he was talking to Joseph. He begged the ruler of Egypt, who was actually his brother in disguise. He said, "You asked us if we had a father or a brother, and we told you the truth. We told you that one of our brothers was dead. We told you that our dead brother's younger brother was the only one left of his mother's sons. You asked us to bring that younger brother to you, and we told you that our father could not live without him. Our father loves Benjamin so much. If he doesn't return home, our father will die; he told us so himself." Then Judah begged, "So please, your highness! Please take me instead. Please let Benjamin go back to his father, and let *me* stay as your slave! I could not bear to watch my father die of sadness!"

Discussion:

In what way was Joseph testing his brothers?

Did Judah pass the test?

Part II: Genesis 45:1-:24

NT: Romans 8:18-39

Joseph was overwhelmed with emotion. He ordered his servants to leave the room quickly, and then he began to cry. He'd held back the tears for as long as he possibly could. Joseph wept so loudly that everyone outside his home could hear him, and soon everyone in the palace had heard about it.

Joseph spoke to his brothers without a translator in the room. He said, "It's me! I'm Joseph! Is my father *really* still alive?"

His brothers were too stunned to speak. They did not know what to believe. Joseph said, "Come closer." Then quietly, so no one outside could hear, he said, "It's me, the brother you sold into slavery. Don't worry! And don't be angry with yourselves about what you did to me. There will be five more years of famine, and God sent me here to save lives. See, it was God, not you, who sent me here! Now go quickly, tell our dad that I am ruler of Egypt. Tell him to come to me. Tell him to bring his children and grandchildren down to live in Goshen and be near me! I will provide for you here."

Joseph hugged Benjamin, and both men cried together. Joseph kissed all his brothers, and he cried over each of them. At last, they were all together!

When Pharaoh heard that Joseph had found his brothers, he was pleased. Joseph was a respected and powerful man, and his family was very welcome in Egypt. Pharaoh told Joseph to send his brothers with wagons for their wives and children. He said, "Tell them not to worry about bringing their things; they will be given all the best things in Egypt."

Joseph sent his brothers home to get their families. He sent them with wagons and with donkeys carrying food and gifts. He gave each of his brothers new clothes, but he gave Benjamin five times as much clothing plus three hundred shekels of silver. Then he warned them as they rode away, "Don't fight on your way home!"

Discussion:

When did Joseph reveal his identity to his brothers?

How did he convince his brothers that he was Joseph?

Why did Joseph give Benjamin more than his other brothers? Why did he tell them not to fight? Was this another test?

Part III: Genesis 45:25-46:27

NT: Acts 26:6-8; Matthew 19:27-29

When the brothers arrived in Canaan, they told their father that Joseph was not only alive but was ruling the land of Egypt. This seemed like an unbelievable story, and Jacob did not believe it at first. When his sons told him everything that Joseph had said, and when they showed him the gifts that Joseph had sent, Jacob was filled with hope. "My son is alive!" he said. "I will go and see him before I die."

Jacob, now called Israel, gathered his entire family. They left from Canaan, traveling toward Egypt, with all their possessions and livestock. When they stopped to camp in Beersheba, Israel built an altar to God. God spoke to him that night, and He called him Jacob. He said, "Don't be afraid of going to Egypt. I will make you a great nation there, and I will bring you back home again. Joseph will be with you when you die."

Israel took his sons and their wives and children and continued on to Egypt. There were sixty-six descendants of Jacob traveling with him—not counting his sons' wives who were also with him.

Discussion:

Did Israel believe that his son was alive?

How many people went to Egypt with Israel?

Part IV: Genesis 46:28-47:12

NT: Hebrews 11:8-10

Israel sent Judah on ahead to get directions to the land where Joseph said they should live. When Joseph heard that his family had arrived in Goshen, he rode in his chariot to meet them. He ran to his father and hugged him, and he cried and cried for a long time. Israel said, "Now I can die happy, because I know you are alive!"

Joseph told his father and brothers that he would go speak to Pharaoh. He would tell Pharaoh that his family had arrived, and he would tell him that they were shepherds who had come with livestock.

"When Pharaoh speaks to you," Joseph said to his father and brothers, "you should also tell him that you are shepherds—just as all your relatives have been. The Egyptians do not like shepherds, so he will send you outside of Egypt to the land of Goshen."

Joseph chose five of his brothers, and he took them to meet Pharaoh. Pharaoh asked them, "What is your job? What do you do for a living?"

They answered and said, "We are shepherds as our fathers were. The famine is terrible in Canaan, and there is nothing for our sheep to eat. Please allow us to settle in Goshen."

Pharaoh spoke to Joseph and said, "Let your family live in Goshen, and if any of them are especially good shepherds, please put them in charge of my flocks as well."

Then Joseph brought his father to meet Pharaoh. Jacob blessed Pharaoh, and Pharaoh asked him how old he was. Jacob told Pharaoh that he was one hundred and thirty years old.

Joseph made sure that his family lived in the best part of the land, just as Pharaoh had said, and he gave them food as well.

Discussion:

Why did Joseph want his family to live in Goshen?

Why did Joseph think that Pharaoh would want them to live in Goshen?

Did Israel's family have a good home in Goshen?

Part V: Genesis 47:13-27

NT: Acts 2:44-46

Joseph continued to sell grain to the people in Egypt and to the people who came from Canaan to buy grain. The famine was terrible for many miles around. When everyone's money was gone, Joseph allowed the people of Egypt to sell their livestock in exchange for grain.

When all their animals were gone, the people had nothing left. They sold themselves and their land in exchange for food. Joseph did not buy the land of Pharaoh's priests, however, because Pharaoh provided for them.

Now Pharaoh owned all the land of Egypt except for the land of the priests. Joseph gave the people seed to plant in their fields, and he told them that they would owe one-fifth of their harvest to Pharaoh. The Egyptians were so grateful for the food that this seemed like a great deal to them.

The Israelites lived in Goshen. They owned land there, and Israel's family grew.

Discussion:

What did the Egyptians do when they ran out of money to buy grain?

What happened to the Israelites as this time?

Vayechi (He lived) –
Genesis 47:28 - 50:26; I Kings 2:1-12

Portion:

Part I: Genesis 47:28-48:22

NT: I Corinthians 15

After arriving in Egypt, Jacob lived seventeen more years. When he felt that his life was almost over, he called for Joseph. "Promise me that you will not bury me in Egypt," he said. "Promise me that you'll bury me where my fathers are buried."

Joseph promised, and Israel praised the Lord that he would not be buried in Egypt.

A little while later, Joseph heard that his father was sick. Joseph took his two sons, Manasseh and Ephraim, and he rode out to Goshen to see Israel.

When Israel saw Joseph, he sat up in bed. He reminded Joseph of God's promise to make a great nation from Israel. Then Israel said, "Your sons, Ephraim and Manasseh, will be counted as my sons. Any children born after them will be yours, and they will inherit through their brothers, but Ephraim and Manasseh will receive an inheritance as my sons. Bring them to me so that I can bless them."

Israel was nearly blind. Joseph brought his sons close so that his father could see them. Joseph bowed low to the ground. He led Manasseh (the older son) to his father's right hand and Ephraim (the younger son) to his father's left hand. Israel crossed his arms so that his right hand was on Ephraim and his left hand was on Manasseh. Then Israel blessed Joseph through his sons. He said, "May the God of my fathers bless these boys. May they be called by the name of Abraham, Isaac, and Israel, and may they fill the earth."

Joseph looked up and saw that his father had crossed his arms. He said, "No, father, Manasseh is the older son and Ephraim is the younger." Israel answered, "I know, son, and they will both be great nations, but the younger will be greater. He will become many nations."

Then to Joseph he said, "God will be with my family after I die. He will take you back to the land of our fathers. I want to give you a special gift that your brothers will not receive, and so to you alone, not to your brothers, I give the piece of land that I took from the Amorites."

Discussion:

Why was it so important to Israel that he not be buried in Egypt?

Why do you think that Israel chose to count Ephraim and Manasseh as his own sons?

Why did Israel (who had been Jacob) cross his arms when blessing the boys?

Part II: Genesis 49:1-28

NT: Revelation 7

All of Israel's sons gathered around him so that he could bless them and prophesy over them before he died.

Israel reminded Reuben of the great power and responsibility he possessed as the first-born. Then he told him that he would no longer prosper because he had sinned against his father's marriage to Bilhah, Rachel's servant.

He spoke to Simeon and Levi, and he reminded them of the terrible crime they committed when they avenged their sister, Dinah. He cursed their anger, and he prophesied that they would be scattered throughout Israel.

Israel praised Judah. He said that his brothers would think well of him and that their children would bow to him. He said that Judah would be above his enemies. He said that Judah would rule and reign until the true king came to rule the nations.

Israel said that Zebulun would live by the sea and become a safe place for ships.

Israel said that Issachar was like a strong donkey living with sheep. Because the land was comfortable, he would willingly work as a servant.

Israel told Dan that he would provide justice and be a judge for all his people. He would be like a snake by the road—ready to bite at whoever tried to cross.

Israel said that Gad would be attacked, but he would fight back and attack his enemies' heels.

Israel said that Asher would grow and harvest rich food fit for royalty.

Israel said that Naphtali would run free like a deer and speak beautiful words.

Israel said that Joseph was a healthy vine whose branches would climb over the wall. He said that archers had tried to destroy him, but God had kept him safe. Again, he reminded

Joseph of all the blessings that God had promised to Abraham, Isaac, and Israel. He placed all those blessings upon Joseph, and he called him a prince.

Israel said that Benjamin was a hungry wolf. He would devour his prey in the morning and divide up the spoils in the evening.

Discussion:

Which son received the greatest blessing? Discuss the blessings.

Part III: Genesis 49:29-50:14

NT: Matthew 22:30-32; John 11:24-35

Then Israel said, "I'm about to die. Bury me with my fathers in the cave that Abraham bought from the Hittite. Abraham and Sarah are buried there. Isaac and Rebekah are there, and I buried Leah there." Then Israel laid down and died.

Joseph threw himself over his father; he cried and kissed him. Then Joseph ordered the Egyptians to prepare his father's body according to Egyptian customs. This took forty days, and all of Egypt mourned for Israel for seventy days.

When the time for mourning was over, Joseph spoke to Pharaoh's assistants. Joseph said, "Please speak to Pharaoh for me. I would like permission to take my father's body to Canaan to bury him like I promised." Pharaoh told Joseph to keep his word. So, Joseph took Israel's body to Canaan, and a very large group of people—Pharaoh's officials and Israel's family—went with him.

When they reached Atad, near the Jordan, the entire group of people stopped and mourned again. They cried loudly, and they stayed and mourned for seven days. When the Canaanites saw the people mourning there, they named the place *Abel Mizraim*, meaning, "mourning of the Egyptians."

Joseph buried his father in the cave in the field of Machpelah, near Mamre, which Abraham had bought. Then they all went back to Egypt.

Discussion:

Why did Joseph ask for his father's body to be prepared by the Egyptians?

Why did all of Egypt mourn for Israel?

Why did Joseph need to ask Pharaoh's permission before he went to bury his father?

Part IV: Genesis 50:15-21

NT: Matthew 6:12-15

After Israel was buried, Joseph's older brothers were worried. They were afraid that Joseph had only been kind to them for their father's sake. Now that Israel was dead, they feared that Joseph would punish them. They sent a note to Joseph saying, "Before dad died, he asked that you forgive us. Please forgive us." When Joseph read the note, he cried.

When his brothers came to him, they fell on the ground in front of him and said, "We are your slaves!" Joseph said, "Don't be afraid of me. You meant to hurt me, but it was God who sent me to Egypt. Don't worry! I will still provide for you and your children."

Discussion:

Why did Joseph's brothers say that they were his slaves?

Why did Joseph say that God had sent him to Egypt?

Part V: Genesis 50:22-26

NT: Hebrews 11:21-22; I Peter 1:3-9

Joseph stayed in Egypt with the rest of his family. He lived long enough to see his great, great, great grandchildren. He died when he was one hundred and ten years old. Before Joseph died, he made the Israelites promise to take his bones with them when they left Egypt. He said, "God will help you. He'll take you back to the Promised Land. Promise me that when you leave you will take my bones with you to Canaan."

Discussion:

Why did Joseph want his bones to return to Canaan?

Shemot (Names) –
Exodus 1:1 - 6:1;
Isaiah 27:6 - 28:13, 29:22-23;
Jeremiah 1:1 - 2:3

Portion:

Part I: Exodus 1:1-22

NT: Matthew 2:15-18

Israel had traveled to Egypt with his sons and their wives and children. Counting Joseph and his sons, Jacob had seventy descendants in Egypt. Many years later, after Israel and his twelve sons and their children were gone, the Israelite people were a large nation that filled the whole land of Goshen.

Egypt now had a new Pharaoh, and the new Pharaoh did not care about Joseph or the reason the Israelites had come to Goshen. He thought there were far too many Israelites. He was afraid of them, and he didn't trust them. "If war breaks out, they will join our enemies. They will fight against us and leave Egypt!" he said.

Pharaoh put slave masters over the Israelites and made them work very hard; the slave masters forced the Israelites to build cities for Pharaoh. The harsher Pharaoh was on the Israelites, however, the stronger they grew and the more children they had. Then Pharaoh had another idea.

Shiphrah and Puah were midwives; they helped the Hebrew women deliver their babies. Pharaoh said to them, "When you are helping a Hebrew woman deliver her baby, and you see that the baby is a boy, kill him."

Pharaoh was a very powerful man, and he expected the midwives to obey him without question. But Shiphrah and Puah feared God much more than they feared Pharaoh. They could not do this horrible thing, and they let the baby boys live.

When Pharaoh heard that the baby boys were living, he called for Shiphrah and Puah again. "Why have you disobeyed me?" he asked.

The midwives answered and said, "The Hebrew women are strong, and they give birth before we get there." God blessed the midwives for their faithfulness, and He gave them families of their own.

Angry that his plan had failed again, Pharaoh came up with a new plan. He ordered his people to throw every Hebrew baby boy into the Nile River.

Discussion:

Why didn't Pharaoh want the Israelites to leave Egypt?

What was Pharaoh's first plan to break down the Israelites?

How did Pharaoh plan to quietly kill the Hebrew baby boys?

What happened when the midwives did not kill the babies?

Part II: Exodus 2:1-25

NT: Romans 12:19

A Levite man married a Levite woman. They had a son and a daughter, and then they had a baby boy. They hid the baby from Pharaoh for three months, but soon he was too big to hide. So, his mother took a basket, and she covered it with tar. She placed her baby boy inside the basket, also called an ark, and she put him in the tall reeds along the bank of the Nile River. As the baby floated there, his sister watched him from a distance.

After a while, Pharaoh's daughter came to the river to bathe. She saw the basket with the baby, and she knew he was a Hebrew. She felt sorry for him.

The baby's sister was still watching. She ran to the princess and asked, "Would you like me to find a Hebrew woman to nurse this baby for you?" The princess told her to find someone quickly and even said that she would pay the woman. The princess named the baby *Moses*, because Moses means "to draw out." Moses's sister ran to get her own mother, so Moses's mother was paid to nurse her own son. When he was older, his birth mother took him back to the palace, and he became the princess's son.

One day, when Moses was grown, he visited the place where his people were working. He watched them work, and he saw them being abused. He saw an Egyptian slave master beating a Hebrew slave, and Moses secretly killed the Egyptian and hid him in the sand.

The next day, Moses tried to stop a fight between two Hebrews. The one in the wrong said, "Are you going to kill *me* like you killed the Egyptian?" Then Moses knew that someone had witnessed his crime, and he was afraid.

When Pharaoh heard what Moses had done, he tried to have him killed. Moses ran from Egypt and went to Midian. When he arrived in Midian, he rested by a well.

Soon, the seven daughters of a Midian priest came to the well with their father's camels. Shepherds came and bullied the girls. Moses saw this, and he came to the girls' rescue. He watered their camels for them. When the girls arrived back at home, their father asked them how they had finished their work so quickly. Then they told him about their rescuer.

"Well, why didn't you bring him back with you?" their father asked, so they invited Moses to come and eat dinner with them.

Moses lived with Jethro, the Midian priest. He married Jethro's daughter, Zipporah. Zipporah had a son, and Moses named him *Gershom*, meaning "foreigner."

During that time, the king of Egypt died. The Israelites were still slaves in Egypt, and they cried out to God. God heard them, and He remembered His promise to Abraham, Isaac, and Jacob.

Discussion:

Who were Moses's parents?

How did Moses's mother save his life?

Who cared for Moses when he was a young baby/toddler?

What happened when Moses saw an Egyptian beating a Hebrew?

Did anyone see Moses kill the Egyptian?

What happened when Pharaoh found out?

Who did Moses meet by a well in Midian?

Who did Moses marry?

Part III: Exodus 3:1-22

NT: John 10:2-4

One day, while he was shepherding Jethro's sheep, Moses led the sheep all the way to Horeb: the mountain of God. There the angel of YHVH appeared to Moses as fire from within a bush. The bush was on fire, but it didn't burn up. Moses went to look at it.

God called to Moses from inside the bush. Moses answered, "Here I am."

"Don't come any closer," God said, "and take off your shoes. You're standing on holy ground. I am the God of your fathers: the God of Abraham, Isaac, and Jacob."

Then Moses hid his face because he was afraid to see God. God said, "I have seen the trouble of your people in Egypt. I am going to rescue them and bring them back to their land: the land where the Canaanites, Hittites, Amorites, Perizzites, Hivites, and Jebusites are living. I am sending *you* to Pharaoh to rescue the Israelites and bring them out of Egypt."

Moses said, "Me? How could someone like me do something so great?"

God said, "I will be with you. You will bring the people back to worship Me right here on this mountain. Then you will know that I have called you."

Moses asked, "What if the Israelites ask who You are? What name should I tell them?"

God spoke to Moses and told him what to say:

"Say, 'I AM has sent me. YHVH, the God of Abraham, Isaac, and Jacob has sent me to you.' This is My Name forever.

Go to the elders of the Israelites; they will listen to you. Then, you and the elders will go before the king. You'll say,

'Let us take a three-day journey to offer sacrifices to YHVH our God.' But the king will not let you go until I make him, so I will work many miracles. When it is time for you to leave Egypt, I will make the Egyptians very generous to you. Every Israelite woman will ask her Egyptian neighbors for gold, silver, and clothing; they will give it to her. You will make Egypt poor, and you will leave it as wealthy people."

Discussion:

Why did Moses walk over to the bush?

What was the first thing God said to Moses?

What did God say would be the sign that Moses was really called by God?

What did God say when Moses asked for His name?

Did Moses want to be used by God to rescue the Israelites?

Part IV: Exodus 4:1-31

NT: I Corinthians 1:18-31

"What if they don't believe that I spoke with You?" Moses asked YHVH.

"What's in your hand?" YHVH asked.

"A staff," Moses replied.

YHVH said, "Throw it on the ground."

Moses obeyed, and the staff became a snake. God told Moses to grab it by the tail, and the snake became a staff again.

"Put your hand inside your coat," YHVH commanded.

Moses put his hand inside his coat. When he took his hand back out, it was covered in the disease of leprosy.

"Put your hand in your coat again," YHVH commanded.

Moses did. When he took it out again, it was healed.

YHVH said, "These are signs so that they can see My power. If they do not believe Me after these signs, take some water from the Nile and pour it onto the ground. It will turn to blood."

"But Lord," Moses said, "I am not a good speaker. I stumble over my words."

"I am the One who gives men their mouths. I will teach you what to say," YHVH answered.

Then Moses said, "YHVH, please forgive me, but won't You please send someone else?"

Now God was frustrated with Moses; He was angry at him. He said, "Your brother, Aaron, can speak well. He is on his way to see you right now. I will help both of you, and I will teach you what to say and do. Aaron will be your mouth, and you will tell him what I say. Take this staff so you can perform the signs with it."

YHVH told Moses that it was now safe for him to go back to Egypt. Moses went to his father-in-law and asked for permission to leave. Jethro agreed, and Moses took his wife and sons and headed to Egypt. YHVH said, "Perform the miracles that I taught you to do. Then say, 'Israel is My first-born son. Because you will not let My son go to worship Me, I will kill your first-born son.'"

While Moses and his wife and sons were camping along the way, YHVH became angry and was ready to kill him. Just then, Zipporah grabbed a flint knife and circumcised her son. She touched Moses's feet with the skin. Then Zipporah told Moses that there was a covenant of blood between them.

While Moses was still on his way to Egypt, Aaron met him in the wilderness because YHVH had told him to go there. Moses told Aaron everything that YHVH had told him. When they arrived in Egypt, Aaron gathered the elders of the Israelites and told them everything that Moses had told him. He performed the miracles that God had told him to perform. When the people heard that YHVH cared about their suffering, they bowed and worshipped God.

Discussion:

When/where did Aaron meet Moses?

Who did YHVH almost kill? Why did He want to kill him?

Part V: Exodus 5:1-6:1

NT: Romans 11:25-27

Moses and Aaron went to Pharaoh. They said, "YHVH is the God of Israel. He wants His people to go and worship Him in the wilderness."

Pharaoh answered and said, "I do not know this YHVH. Why should I obey Him?"

Moses and Aaron said, "Our God has met with us. He told us to go three days into the wilderness and offer sacrifices to Him. If we do not go, there will be consequences."

Then Pharaoh said, "The people need to work! Don't stop them from working."

That same day, Pharaoh told the slave masters, "Don't give the Hebrews any straw to make their bricks. Now they will have to get their own straw *and* make the bricks! But be sure they make as many bricks as before." When the Israelites could not make as many bricks as before, the slave masters beat them.

Now the Israelites were angry at Moses and Aaron because things were worse for them than they had been before.

Moses went to YHVH and said, "Why have You brought me here? Now things are worse! You have not rescued your people at all."

Then YHVH answered him and said, "Now you will see My deliverance and My mighty hand! Because of Me, Pharaoh will drive My people out of Egypt!"

Discussion:

Why did Pharaoh give the Israelites so much work?

What did Pharaoh tell the slave masters to stop giving the Hebrews?

What did God promise Moses?

Va'era (I appeared) –
Exodus 6:2 - 9:35; Ezekiel 28:25 - 29:21

Portion:

Part I: Exodus 6:2-27

NT: Matthew 11:28-30

God spoke to Moses and said, "My name is YHVH. Abraham, Isaac, and Jacob knew Me as the Almighty God. Did they not know Me as YHVH? I made a covenant with them, and I promised them the land of Canaan where they lived as strangers. Now I have heard their descendants crying out, and I have remembered My covenant.

Give the Israelites a message from Me. Say from Me, 'I am YHVH. I will bring you out of your slavery. I will work miracles in order to redeem you. I will take you as My own people, and I will be your God. When these things are done, you will know that I am YHVH. I will bring you to the land that I gave to your fathers.'"

Moses went to the Israelites with this message, but because they were angry and tired, they didn't listen.

YHVH told Moses to go to Pharaoh, but Moses said, "My lips are uncircumcised. Why would Pharaoh listen to me when my own people won't even listen to me?"

Moses and Aaron were descendants of Israel.

Reuben, Israel's first-born, had four sons.

Simeon, Israel's second born, had six sons.

Levi, Israel's third born, had three sons: Gershon, Kohath, and Merari.

Gershon's sons were Libni and Shimei.

Kohath's sons were Amram, Izhar, Hebron, and Uzziel.

Merari's sons were Mahli and Mushi.

Amram married Kohath's sister, Jochebed, and they had two sons: Aaron and Moses.

Izhar's sons were Korah, Nepheg, and Zikri.

Uzziel's sons were Mishael, Elzaphan, and Sithri.

Aaron married Elisheba, daughter of Amminadab and sister of Nashon. Their sons were Nadab and Abihu, Eleazar and Ithamar. Korah's sons were Assir, Elkanah, and Abiasaph. These were the clans of Korah.

Aaron's son Eleazar married one of Putiel's daughters. Phinehas was their son.

Aaron and Moses are the ones YHVH talked to and said, "Bring the Israelites out of Egypt."

Discussion:

Who did YHVH tell Moses that He was?

What did God tell Moses about the reason He was rescuing the Israelites from Egypt?

Why would the Israelites not listen to Moses?

Do you remember the prophecies given to Reuben, Simeon, and Levi by their father, Israel?

Three generations later, what do you see?

Part II: Exodus 6:28-7:13

NT: John 12:30-41

YHVH said to Moses, "I have made you like a god to Pharaoh. Aaron will be your prophet. Say everything that I command you to say, but I will harden Pharaoh's heart; he will not hear you. In the end, when I bring the Israelites out of Egypt, everyone will see that I am YHVH."

Moses and Aaron obeyed God, and they went to speak to Pharaoh. When Pharaoh asked for a miracle, Moses told Aaron to throw down his staff just as God had commanded. Aaron's staff became a snake.

Pharaoh called his magicians and ordered them to do the same. They did, but the snake from Aaron's staff swallowed up the snakes from the magicians' staffs. Even still, Pharaoh was not impressed. Pharaoh's heart was hard toward God—just as YHVH had said.

Discussion:

Why was Pharaoh's heart hard toward God?

Part III: Exodus 7:14-24

NT: Matthew 13:10-16

YHVH said to Moses, "Go to Pharaoh in the morning while he's at the Nile River." Moses obeyed everything YHVH commanded. Moses said to Pharaoh, "YHVH sent me to tell you: 'Let My people go so that they may worship Me in the wilderness.' But you have not listened. YHVH says, 'You will know that I am YHVH.' With this staff in my hand, I will change the water in this river to blood. Everything in the river will die."

Moses told Aaron to take his staff and to stretch it over the waters of Egypt. All the water turned to blood—even the water in pitchers and pots. Then Pharaoh's magicians worked the same miracle, and Pharaoh's heart was hard. No one could drink the water from the river, so the Egyptians dug alongside the river to try to find water to drink.

Discussion:

What was the first plague that God brought upon the Egyptians?

Why would Pharaoh want his magicians to work the same wonders—even at the expense of fresh water?

Part IV: Exodus 7:25-8:32

NT: Revelation 8:6-9:12

Seven days after God turned the waters of Egypt to blood, God told Moses to go back to Pharaoh. Moses obeyed. He said, "YHVH says, 'Let My people go and worship Me. If you do not, I will send a plague of frogs. Frogs will cover the whole land of

Egypt. They will be in your rooms, in your food, and even in your beds.' "

Moses told Aaron to stretch his staff over the streams of Egypt as God had commanded, and Aaron did. Frogs came out of the water and flooded the land. Then Pharaoh's magicians brought more frogs just to prove that they could.

Pharaoh called for Moses and said, "Pray to YHVH and ask Him to take away these frogs. I will let your people go and sacrifice to Him."

Moses answered and said, "When would you like me to pray to God? You pick the time."

"Tomorrow," Pharaoh replied.

Moses prayed to YHVH, and all the frogs on the land died. Only the frogs in the river lived. When Pharaoh was no longer bothered by the frogs, his heart became hard again. He would not listen to Moses and Aaron, and he would not let the people go.

Then YHVH said to Moses, "Tell Aaron to stretch out his staff and to strike the dust of the ground. All of Egypt will be filled with gnats." Aaron did this, and gnats were everywhere—on people and on animals. When Pharaoh's magicians tried to make gnats, they could not do it. Even still, Pharaoh would not listen.

Then YHVH said to Moses, "Go to Pharaoh early in the morning when he is by the river. Tell him again for Me, 'Let My people go so they may worship Me. If you do not, I will send a plague of flies. Flies will be on everyone and everything in Egypt, but they will not be in the land of Goshen where My people live.'"

Pharaoh would not listen, and flies filled Egypt and ruined the land. Then Pharaoh called for Moses and Aaron. "Sacrifice to YHVH in the land of Egypt!" Pharaoh said.

Moses answered, "No, that will not work. The Egyptians will not understand the way we sacrifice to our God, and they will stone us. We must make a three-day journey as YHVH has commanded."

Pharaoh said, "Then go, but do not go very far. Now pray for me."

Moses answered and said, "I will pray to YHVH, and He will take away the flies. Be sure to keep your word!"

Moses prayed, and YHVH took away the flies. But as soon as the flies were gone, Pharaoh's heart was hard again. He would not let the people go.

Discussion:

What was the second plague that God brought upon Egypt?

Why did God cause the frogs to die?

What was the third plague God brought upon Egypt?

What was the fourth plague God brought upon Egypt?

What was the first plague that affected only the Egyptians and not the Israelites in Goshen?

Part V: Exodus 9:1-35
NT: James 5:1-11

YHVH gave Moses another message for Pharaoh. He said, "Let My people go and worship Me. If you will not let them, I will bring terrible sickness to all your livestock, but I will protect the animals that belong to the Israelites."

Pharaoh did not let the people go, and the next day the Egyptian's animals were sick with terrible diseases. Pharaoh sent men into the Israelites' land and saw that their animals were healthy. Even still, Pharaoh would not let the Israelites go.

Then YHVH told Moses and Aaron, "Take a handful of ash and throw it into the air while Pharaoh is watching. It will become a fine dust, and it will spread throughout the land. All the

Egyptians and all the Egyptian's animals will be covered with painful sores."

Moses and Aaron obeyed God, and the Egyptians suffered with terrible sores. Still, Pharaoh would not listen to Moses.

Then YHVH said to Moses, "Go to Pharaoh early in the morning. Give him this message: 'Let My people go and worship Me! If you don't, I will really show you My power. I could have already wiped Egypt from the face of the earth, but I am using this situation. News of the wonders that happen here will spread throughout all the world. At this time tomorrow, I will send the worst hailstorm that has ever come to Egypt. Stay inside, and bring your livestock inside. Anyone caught in the storm will die.'"

Moses stretched his staff over Egypt, and YHVH sent lighting and hail like the land had never seen. But in the land of Goshen, where the Israelites lived, there was no hail.

Some of Pharaoh's officials had brought their slaves and their animals inside. For those who didn't, every person and animal they owned was killed by the pelting hail.

Pharaoh called for Moses. He said, "I have sinned this time. YHVH is right, and we are wrong. Pray to God, and ask Him to stop the hail; I will let the Israelites go."

When Moses prayed, YHVH stopped the hail. Then Pharaoh's heart was hardened again.

Discussion:

What was the fifth plague God brought upon the Egyptians?

What was the sixth plague God brought upon the Egyptians?

What was the seventh plague God brought upon Egypt?

What merciful warning did God give to Pharaoh through Moses?

Bo (Go) –
Exodus 10:1 - 13:16; Jeremiah 46:13-28

Portion:

Part I: Exodus 10:1-11:10

NT: Matthew 10:12-16

YHVH hardened Pharaoh's heart. He did this so that everyone could see the wonders of God as He performed His miracles in Egypt. YHVH sent Moses to Pharaoh with a message. He said, "How long will you refuse to be humble? Let My people go so that they may worship Me. If you do not, I will send a plague of locusts like you have never seen. Everything that the hail did not destroy will be eaten by the locust."

Pharaoh's officials begged him to let the Israelites go. Pharaoh agreed, but he wanted to know which of the Israelites would be going. When Moses answered, "We will all be going—along with all our animals," Pharaoh became very angry.

"No! I can tell that you are planning to run away! You asked to take a three-day journey to worship God. Only the men may go and do that," Pharaoh said.

So YHVH commanded Moses to stretch his staff over Egypt. Locust swarmed through the land and ate everything in sight.

Pharaoh called for Moses again; he begged Moses to pray and to ask God to take the locust away. Moses prayed, and YHVH listened. But Pharaoh's heart was still hard; he would not let the people go.

Moses stretched his staff over Egypt again as YHVH commanded. A thick and terrifying darkness covered the land of Egypt so the Egyptians could not see their hands in front of their faces. In Goshen, where the Israelites lived, there was light.

Pharaoh called to Moses because he wanted to make a deal. He said, "You may all go to worship, the men and the women, the boys and the girls…just leave your animals behind."

Moses answered and said, "We must take our animals with us. We need them for sacrifices, and we won't know which ones we need until we get there."

Pharaoh was angry. He would not let the Israelites go. He told Moses to leave and to never come back into his presence.

Moses answered and said, "Fine. I will not come to you again, but YHVH will bring one more plague to Egypt. Around midnight, YHVH will go through Egypt and kill every first-born.

From the first-born son of Pharaoh to the first-born sons of your animals, all of them will die. The Israelites will not have any troubles. You will see that YHVH sets His people apart from Egypt. When this happens, you will order us to leave."

Then Moses left Pharaoh's presence.

Discussion:

Who was Pharaoh willing to let go into the wilderness to worship?

Why was Pharaoh unwilling to let everyone and their animals go?

What was the eighth plague God brought upon Egypt?

What was the ninth plague God brought upon Egypt?

What did Moses tell Pharaoh that the tenth and last plague would be?

Part II: Exodus 12:1-30

NT: Matthew 26

YHVH told Moses and Aaron, "This month is the first month of your year. Tell everyone that on the tenth day of this month each man is to pick out a lamb. If his family is too small to eat a whole lamb, he should plan to share a lamb with his neighbors. These lambs or goats should be perfect one-year-old males. Each family will take care of their lamb until the fourteenth day of this month.

Just before evening on the fourteenth day, all the people will kill their lambs. Then they will take some of the blood and put it around their doorways. On that same night, they will roast the lamb over fire and eat it inside their homes. They will eat it with bitter herbs and bread made without yeast. They must eat it quickly, and they must not leave any leftovers. Any leftovers must be burned in the fire. This is the Lord's Passover.

On that night, I will pass through Egypt and kill the first-born of people and animals, but where I see blood on the door, I will pass over. No plague will touch you.

This is a day you should remember forever because this is the day I will bring you out of Egypt. Celebrate this day throughout all your generations by eating bread made without yeast for seven days. On the first day of this celebration, you will remove all the yeast from your home. You may prepare food, but otherwise you should rest and not work on the first day of this feast. No matter where you live, no one is allowed to eat any yeast during this Festival of Unleavened Bread. If they do, they will be cut off from Israel.

Moses called together the leaders of Israel and told them all that God had said. He told them to pick out a lamb for their families, and he told them when to kill and eat it. He told them to use hyssop as a brush and to put the lamb's blood on their doorframes. He said that YHVH would see the blood and pass over, not allowing their first-borns to be killed.

Then Moses said to the people, "You will celebrate this same feast when you have entered the Promised Land. You will remember the Passover night throughout all your generations, and you will teach your children about it."

The people obeyed YHVH. Then at midnight, on the fourteenth of the month, YHVH came through Egypt as He had said. Wherever blood was on the doorpost, YHVH passed over. Every first-born of Egypt died.

Discussion:

What did God call the month they were in when He spoke to Moses about the final plague?

What did God tell Moses to do on the tenth day of this month?

What did God tell Moses to do on the fourteenth day of this month?

When God saw the blood on the doorpost, what did He do?

Part III: Exodus 12:31-42

NT: Hebrews 11:28; Galatians 3:16-18

While it was still night, Pharaoh called for Moses and Aaron. He said, "Leave Egypt immediately. Take everyone and everything that belongs to you, and leave. Say a blessing for me."

The Israelites left quickly before their bread had a chance to rise. They carried the dough on their shoulders wrapped in clothing. Just as YHVH had commanded, Moses told the Israelites to ask the Egyptians for gold, silver, and clothing. The Egyptians gave the Israelites whatever they asked for because YHVH had made them feel generous toward Israel.

The Israelites began walking from Rameses to Sukkoth. There were six hundred thousand men on foot along with their wives and children. Many other people followed the Israelites out of Egypt as well. In addition to all the people, they also journeyed with large herds of livestock. When they camped, they baked the unleavened bread they had carried out of Egypt.

When the Israelites came out of Egypt, it had been 430 years since Abraham arrived in Canaan.

Discussion:

After the final plague, did Moses ask Pharaoh's permission to leave?

What time of day was it when the Israelites walked out of Egypt?

Part IV: Exodus 12:43-51

NT: I Corinthians 5:7-8; John 19:31-37

YHVH said to Moses and Aaron, "The Passover meal must be eaten inside. Do not break any of the bones of the animal. All of Israel must celebrate the Passover, but no one outside of Israel is allowed to eat it. Your slaves may eat it, but they must be circumcised first. A foreigner who wants to celebrate YHVH's Passover must be circumcised along with all the males in his home. The same Law applies to those who are born as Israelites and those who join themselves to Israel."

Discussion:

What were the requirements for eating the Passover?

Part V: Exodus 13:1-16

NT: Luke 2:1-23

YHVH spoke to Moses, and Moses commanded the people. He said, "Today, in the month of Aviv, we are leaving Egypt. Do not eat any yeast. When you enter the land that YHVH gives you, the land He promised to your fathers, you will celebrate this Feast of Unleavened Bread. When your son asks you why you do this, tell him that you do this because of what YHVH did for us in Egypt.

Once you have entered the Promised Land, you must give YHVH every first-born male: man and animal. When your son asks you, 'What does this mean?' remind him that YHVH killed the first-born in Egypt in order to rescue us. This is why we sacrifice every first-born ram and redeem every first-born son by sacrificing a lamb in his place."

Discussion:

What does it mean to redeem a first-born clean animal?

What does it mean to redeem a first-born son?

Beshalach (After he had let go) – Exodus 13:17 - 17:16; Judges 4:4 - 5:31

Portion:

Part I: Exodus 13:17-14:4

NT: John 16:13

When Pharaoh let the Israelites go, God did not lead them out by the shortest way. That would have taken them through the Philistines' land, and war might have discouraged the people and made them want to go back to Egypt. God led the people to the desert near the Red Sea. Moses took the bones of Joseph with them—just as Joseph had made his people promise.

After leaving their first camp, Sukkoth, the Israelites camped at Etham on the edge of the desert. YHVH went ahead of them. He guided them in a pillar of fire by night and a pillar of cloud by day.

Then YHVH told Moses, "Tell the people to go back between the sea and the mountains of Migdol. Pharaoh will think you are confused. He will think you have become trapped by the desert. He will come after you, but I will get the glory. Then the Egyptians will know, once and for all, that I am YHVH."

The Israelites obeyed.

Discussion:

Did YHVH lead the Israelites on the shortest route out of Egypt? Why?

Why did God tell the Israelites to go back between Migdol and the sea?

Part II: Exodus 14:5-31

NT: I Thessalonians 5:1-28

When Pharaoh saw that the Israelites were gone, he and his officials changed their minds. "Why have we let our slaves go? What will we do without them?" they said. Pharaoh rode in his chariot, and his many officers rode in their chariots. Pharaoh's entire army followed the Israelites—including six hundred of Pharaoh's best chariots.

When the Israelites saw the Egyptians coming, they were terrified. They cried to YHVH. "It would have been better to be slaves than to die in this desert!" they complained to Moses.

Moses answered the people and said, "The Egyptians you see today, you will never see again! YHVH will deliver you. Be still and wait."

YHVH said to Moses, "Why are you crying out to Me? Just go forward! Stretch your staff over the sea, and I will make a dry path through it. The Egyptians will follow you, and I will have the glory."

The angel of God who had been leading the Israelites went behind them to guard them instead. The pillar of cloud moved behind them, too, so the Egyptians could not go near the Israelites. All night long, the pillar left the Egyptians in darkness while it gave light to the Israelites' side.

Moses stretched his hand over the sea, and a strong east wind blew all night long. The wind blew the water into two high walls with a path of dry ground between them. In the morning, the Israelites walked through the sea. The Egyptians followed them. After they had been walking all day, YHVH confused the Egyptians. He broke their chariot wheels so that they had trouble driving. The Egyptians panicked because they knew YHVH was fighting for the Israelites.

Then YHVH commanded Moses to stretch his hand over the sea again, and the waters began to flow back over the Egyptians and their chariots and their horses. By morning, the waters had covered the Egyptians, but the Israelites were safe on the other side.

Discussion:

Why did Pharaoh and his army follow the Israelites?

What did the Israelites say when they saw the Egyptians coming?

What protected the Israelites from the Egyptians?

How did the Israelites cross the sea?

What happened to the Egyptians who followed them?

Part III: Exodus 15:1-27

NT: Revelation 15:2-4

Moses and the Israelites sang a song to YHVH. Miriam, Moses's sister, grabbed a tambourine and led the women dancing in the song of praise!

1. I will sing unto the Lord for He has triumphed gloriously
The horse and rider thrown into the sea.
I will sing unto the Lord for He has triumphed gloriously
Our mighty Lord has crushed the enemy.

Chorus:

The Lord, my God, my strength my song
Has now become my victory.
The Lord, my God, my strength my song
Has now become my victory.

The Lord is God and I will praise Him
My father's God and I will exalt Him.
The Lord is God and I will praise Him
My father's God and I will exalt Him!

2. I will sing unto the Lord for He has triumphed gloriously
And all who hear of His great power will fear.
I will sing unto the Lord for He has triumphed gloriously
YHVH will bring His people forth from here.

3. I will sing unto the Lord for He has triumphed gloriously
He'll lead us to the land that is our home.
I will sing unto the Lord for He has triumphed gloriously
He's bought us and He's going to take us home.

After crossing the Red Sea, Moses led the Israelites into the Desert of Shur. They traveled for three days without finding any water. Then they came to a place they called *Marah*, meaning "bitter," and they could not drink the water there because it was bitter.

Moses prayed to YHVH because the people were thirsty and complaining. YHVH showed Moses a branch, and Moses threw that branch into the water. Then the water was sweetened, and they could drink it.

YHVH tested them there, and He gave them a command. He said, "If you are careful to obey YHVH, I will keep you healthy. You will not have any of the diseases that I brought to the Egyptians. I am YHVH who heals you."

Next, the Israelites came to Elim where there were twelve springs and seventy palm trees. The Israelites camped near the water.

Discussion:

Moses praised YHVH for leading them where?

How did Moses sweeten the bitter water?

How many days did the Israelites travel without finding water?

What did God promise the Israelites in exchange for their obedience?

Part IV (Exodus 16:1-36):

The Israelites camped in the Desert of Sin, which is half-way between Elim and Sinai. It was the fifteenth day of the second month, and they had been free from slavery in Egypt for one month. They were hungry. The Israelites cried out to Moses for food, and they wished they were back in Egypt.

YHVH told Moses that He would send food. Moses and Aaron said to the Israelites, "YHVH will provide food for you. You will know that it was God who sent it when you are eating meat in the evening and bread in the morning. You're not whining at me; you're whining at YHVH." The Israelites looked toward the desert, and they saw the glory of YHVH in the cloud.

That evening, quail covered the Israelites' camp so they had plenty of meat to eat, and in the morning they found a strange layer of dew on the ground. The dew left what looked like thin flakes of frost that tasted sweet like bread made with honey. They said, "Manna?" which means, "What is it?"

Moses told them that the manna was for bread. They were commanded to gather it every morning: one omer for each person in their tent. They were not supposed to gather more than they could eat. When they measured it, those who gathered a lot had just the right amount, and those who gathered a little had just the right amount. If they left manna overnight in their tents, it would attract worms and stink. On the sixth day, however, they were commanded to gather two omers so they would have something to eat on the seventh day. The manna gathered on the sixth day would not go bad overnight because God did not send manna on the seventh day: Shabbat. YHVH commanded the people to rest on the seventh day. YHVH also commanded Moses to save an omer of manna in a jar so that future generations could see it.

Discussion:

What two things did YHVH give the Israelites to eat in the wilderness?

What happened to the manna if they left it in their tents overnight?

What was the exception to this rule?

Part V: Exodus 17:1-16

NT: II Corinthians 8:1-15

The Israelites traveled from place to place and camped where YHVH commanded. When they camped at Rephidim, there was no water for them to drink. Moses called the place Massah and Meribah because of the people's complaining. They fought and argued and cried to Moses for water. Moses asked God what to do. YHVH said to Moses, "Stand in front of the people with your staff in your hand. I will stand on the rock at Horeb. Strike the rock, and water will pour out for the people." Moses obeyed, and the people had water.

The Amalekites came to Rephidim and attacked the Israelites there. Moses commanded Joshua to lead an army against them, and Moses stood on a hill with his staff raised in his hands. The armies battled below. As long as Moses's arms were raised, the Israelites were victorious. If Moses's arms began to fall, the Amalekites would begin to win. So, Aaron and Hur sat Moses on a rock and held his arms up for him. Joshua's army defeated the Amalekites.

YHVH told Moses to write a message on a scroll and to make sure Joshua heard the message. He said, "I will completely erase the Amalekites from the earth."

Moses built an altar to YHVH. He named it YHVH Nissi, "The Lord is my banner," because YHVH raised His hand and swore to destroy the Amalekites.

Discussion:

How did God provide water for the people where there was none?

What happened when Moses's hands began to fall? Why?

Yitro (Jethro) –
Exodus 18:1 - 20:23; Isaiah 6:1 - 7:6, 9:5-7

Portion:

Part I: Exodus 18:1-12

NT: Mark 12:32-34

Moses's wife, Zipporah, and their sons, Gershom and Eliezar, had not traveled to Egypt with Moses. Along the way from Midian to Egypt, Moses sent them back to Midian. Jethro, Moses's father-in-law, had welcomed his daughter and grandsons into his home. When Jethro heard that YHVH had freed the Israelites from slavery in Egypt, he took Moses's wife and sons and traveled to meet Moses in the wilderness. Moses was happy to see his father-in-law. The two men talked and talked about all the wonders YHVH had done for the Israelites in rescuing them from the Egyptians. Jethro could see that YHVH was greater than all other gods. He said, "Praise YHVH who rescued you from the Egyptians! Now I know that YHVH is greater than all gods." Jethro offered a sacrifice to God, and Aaron and all the leaders of Israel came and ate a meal with Jethro, Moses's father-in-law.

Discussion:

What god did Jethro serve?

What did Jethro say when he heard about what YHVH had done?

Part II: Exodus 18:13-27

NT: Titus 1:6-11; Acts 6:1-7

The next day, Jethro watched Moses as he worked from sunup to sundown giving advice to and solving arguments between the many, many Israelites. The people all came to Moses to hear from God.

"You're working much too hard!" Jethro told Moses. "You will wear yourself out." Moses listened to Jethro, and Jethro said, "You must speak to God for the people, and you must teach them how to serve Him, but put leaders in charge of thousands, leaders in charge of hundreds, and pick small group leaders too. These men can deal with the everyday problems. The leaders of small groups can take their bigger problems to the leaders of hundreds, and the leaders of hundreds can take difficult problems to the leaders of thousands. If the leaders of thousands cannot decide on a solution, they can bring the problem to you. You will only have to solve the problems that cannot be solved without your help."

Moses agreed with Jethro, and he did what he said. Then Moses sent Jethro back to his home in Midian.

Discussion:

What advice did Jethro give to Moses?

Part III: Exodus 19:1-15

NT: I Peter 2:1-10

After leaving Rephidim, the Israelites traveled to Sinai. On the first day of the third month, the Israelites reached the Desert of Sinai. They camped in front of the mountain.

Moses went up the mountain to talk to God; YHVH talked to him and gave him a message for the Israelites. He said, "You've seen what I did to the Egyptians and how I carried you out on eagles' wings. Obey Me, and though the whole earth is Mine, *you* will be My special treasure: a kingdom of priests and a holy nation to Me."

Moses told the people what YHVH said, and they answered, "Yes, we will do whatever YHVH says!"

Then YHVH told Moses, "I will come in a thick cloud. The people will hear Me speaking to you, so they will never doubt you. Tell the people to wash their clothes and to be clean for Me. On the third day, I will come down on Mount Sinai so that all the people can see. Mark out limits around the mountain. Make sure no one comes near the mountain until you hear the long trumpet blast. Anyone who touches the mountain will have to be killed."

Moses went down the mountain to the people. He told them to clean themselves and to get ready for the third day.

Discussion:

What did YHVH tell the Israelites they would be to Him if they obeyed Him?

What did the people say when Moses gave them the message (telling them to obey God and to be His special people)?

On what day did YHVH say He was going to speak to the people?

What would YHVH do to help the people trust Moses?

Part IV: Exodus 19:16-25

NT: Hebrews 12:18-24

On the morning of the third day, the people saw thunder, lighting, and a thick cloud covering the top of the mountain. All the Israelites were very afraid. They heard a loud trumpet blast, and then Moses led the people to the base of the mountain to meet with God. The top of the mountain looked like a furnace. The mountain smoked and trembled. The sound of the trumpet grew louder and louder. Moses spoke, and God thundered back.

God called Moses to the top of the mountain, so Moses climbed up to meet Him. When Moses reached the top, YHVH said, "Go down, and warn the people not to rush toward the mountain to meet Me."

Moses answered YHVH and said, "They can't come near the mountain; You told me to put limits around it and to let them know it was holy."

YHVH answered, "Go down and get Aaron. Bring him back with you, but be sure the priests and the people know that they cannot come up to see Me."

Moses went down and spoke to the people.

Discussion:

Did YHVH want the people to come near Him?

Part V: Exodus 20:1-23

NT: Mark 10:18-24; Matthew 5:21-30

The mountain boomed as YHVH spoke these words:

"I am YHVH who rescued you from your slavery. Do not have any other gods or put anything before Me.

Do not make an idol of any image. I am jealous, and you will not bow to anything or anyone but Me.

My name, YHVH, is holy. Do not misuse it.

Remember to keep the Sabbath day holy. Do not work on the Sabbath, and do not cause anyone or any animal to work. I have blessed the Sabbath and set it apart.

Honor your father and mother, and you will live a long life.

Do not murder.

Do not commit adultery.

Do not steal.

Do not give a false testimony.

Do not want things that belong to someone else. Be content with what you have."

The people were very afraid because God spoke through thunder and lighting. They saw the smoke, and they heard the trumpet. They cried out to Moses and said, "*You* speak to us! We will listen. If God speaks to us, we will die!"

Moses told the people, "Do not be afraid. God has come to test you. The fear of Him should keep you from sinning."

The people stayed back, and Moses went up toward God. Then YHVH spoke to Moses and said, "Remind the Israelites that they have heard Me from heaven; I have told them not to make any gods or idols."

Discussion:

Did YHVH want to speak to the people? Did the people want to hear directly from God?

What was the first commandment YHVH spoke to them?

Mishpatim (Rulings) –
Exodus 21:1 - 24:18; Jeremiah 33:25-26, 34:8-22

Portion:

Part I: Exodus 21:1-36

NT: Matthew 5:38-48, 15:1-20

YHVH spoke to Moses and said, "Give these commands to the people:

If you buy a Hebrew servant, the price is for six years. After six years, you must let him go free. If he brought a wife with him, his wife and children will leave with him. If you gave him a wife, his wife and children are still yours. If the servant says, 'I love my master! I love my wife and children, and I want to stay here!' then he can agree to stay. He will then be your servant for life.

If a father sells his daughter as a servant who is married to her master, she will not go free after six years. If her master does not want her to be his wife, he must let her family buy her back. He may not sell her to someone else. If he chose her as a wife for his son, he must treat her exactly as he would treat his own daughter. If he marries another woman after he has married her, he must not take any of her rights and privileges away just because he now has a new wife. If he does not provide her with food, clothing, and the rights of a wife, he must allow her to go free without payment.

Anyone who kills another person on purpose is to be put to death. If the killing is an accident, the guilty person may run and hide in a place that I will choose.

Anyone who attacks their own father or mother will be put to death.

Anyone who kidnaps will be put to death.

Anyone who curses their father or mother will be put to death.

If two people are fighting and one is injured but does not die, the one who did the injuring will pay the injured person enough money to cover their lost pay. He will take care of the injured person until he is completely well and is ready to go back to work.

Anyone who beats their slave to death will be punished.

If a pregnant woman is injured and she goes into labor, there will be no punishment if the baby is alright. The guilty person will be charged whatever amount of money the husband asks as long as the judge thinks it's fair. But if the baby dies or is injured, the one at fault will be punished. There will be serious punishment for serious injury.

If a slave owner hits his slave so that he loses his eyesight, tooth, etc., the slave owner must let him go free to make up for what he has lost.

If a bull kills a man or woman, son or daughter, the bull is to be stoned and not eaten. The owner will not be punished unless he knew that the bull had a habit of charging. If he knew this and did not keep his bull penned up, the owner will be put to death as well. The family of the victim may ask for money instead of the death penalty. If the bull kills a slave, the bull must be stoned, and the bull's owner must pay thirty shekels of silver.

If someone digs a large hole and does not cover it well, and if another man's livestock falls into it, the owner of the hole must pay for the dead animal.

If one man's bull kills another man's bull, the owners will divide the meat of the dead animal. They will also sell the live one and split the money. However, if the owner of the live bull knew that his bull had a habit of charging, he must trade his live animal for the dead one."

Discussion:

What did YHVH say would happen if a slave owner knocked out his slave's tooth?

What did YHVH say would happen if one man's bull killed another man's bull?

Part II: Exodus 22:1-15

NT: Luke 19:8-9

"If someone steals a sheep or ox and then kills or sells it so he cannot give it back, he must pay five times as many oxen and four times as many sheep as he took. If the stolen animal is still alive, he must pay back double.

A thief must pay back what he has stolen plus the amount of the fine. If he cannot afford to do this, he must be sold for payment instead.

If a thief comes in at night and surprises the owner, the owner will not be punished if he kills the burglar. If it is daylight, the burglar can be forced to pay back what he has taken. The homeowner must not kill him.

If someone lets his livestock eat from another man's field, he must pay for what his animals have eaten. He must pay from the best of his own field or vineyard.

If a fire starts and crops are ruined, the one who started the fire must pay for the damage.

Someone may hand his neighbor something valuable and say, "Here, please keep this in a safe place for me!" If robbers break in and steal the valuable thing, the thief will pay back double. If it cannot be proven that there actually was a robber, the two neighbors will go to court to prove what has happened. Whoever the judge says is guilty will pay double to the other.

If someone borrows an animal and it is injured while they have it, the borrower will pay for the animal. If the owner is with the animal when it is injured, the borrower will not pay. If the animal was rented, the rental price will pay for the injury of the animal."

Discussion:

If a man sees another man stealing his cow from outside his window, what should he do (emphasis on "see," because it is daylight)?

If a man hears another man breaking into his house at night, what can he do?

If a farmer lets his animals roam free in his neighbor's garden, what must he do?

Part III: Exodus 22:16-31

NT: James 1:27; Acts 23:1-11

"If a man sleeps with a woman who is not married, he must pay the bride-price set by her father and must marry her immediately. If the father will not let him marry her, he must still pay the bride-price.

Anyone who practices witchcraft will die. Anyone who sleeps with an animal in the way meant for husbands and wives will die. Anyone who sacrifices to another god will die.

You were foreigners in Egypt. Never treat anyone the way you were treated by the Egyptians.

Do not take advantage of a widow or orphan. I will hear them when they cry out to Me, and I will make your wife a widow and your children orphans.

If you lend money to the needy, do not charge interest. It is not a business deal. If you take a man's coat as a promise that your money will be paid back, do not keep it until dark. If he is cold and he cries out to Me, I will hear him.

Do not speak against God or curse your rulers.

Do not hold back offerings.

Give Me all your first-born males on the eighth day.

You are not like other people. I have set you apart and called you holy. Do not eat meat killed by wild beasts. Give it to the dogs."

Discussion:

What does it mean to give YHVH a first-born son?

Who did YHVH command the Israelites not to act like?

Part IV: Exodus 23:1-33

NT: Mark 12:30-31; James 2:1-13

"Do not spread false information, and do not testify to protect a guilty person.

Do not join a crowd in doing wrong. Do not side with the crowd. Do not show favoritism to a poor person. Simply tell the truth and do right.

If you see your enemy's livestock wandering away or trapped under its load, do not pretend you don't see. Go and help.

Be careful to do right. Treat the poor fairly. Do not put an innocent person to death.

Do not take money for being a witness. Bribes keep people from seeing straight.

Remember, you were slaves in Egypt. You know what it feels like. Do not mistreat anyone.

Plant and harvest for six years, and let the land rest on the seventh year. The poor may eat from it on the seventh year.

Rest on the seventh day. Do not work, and do not cause anyone or any animal to work on the Sabbath.

Be careful of everything I have said. Do not call out to other gods.

Three times a year, I want you to celebrate a festival in My honor. Celebrate the Feast of Unleavened Bread in the first month of the year. That is when you came out of Egypt. Do not come to the feast without an offering. Next, celebrate the First Fruits of your harvest. Lastly, celebrate the Feast of Sukkot when you harvest your fields at the end of the year. These three times a year, every Israelite man must stand before Me.

Do not offer a blood sacrifice with leavened bread or with anything containing yeast.

The fat from the festival meat should not be kept overnight.

Bring the best of your first fruits to God.

Do not cook a baby goat in his mother's milk.

I am sending My Messenger ahead of you to guard you and to bring you to the place I have prepared for you. Do not disobey Him; He has My Name. If you obey Him, I will be an enemy to all your enemies. Little by little, I will drive out the Amorites, Hittites, Perizzites, Canaanites, Hivites and Jebusites until you are a large enough nation to fill the whole Promised Land. When you live in the land, do not follow the ways or worship the gods of your enemies. Break down their idols. Worship YHVH, and you will be healthy and fed. I will give you long life. The land from the Red Sea to the Mediterranean Sea, from the desert to the Euphrates, will all be yours. You must not make a covenant with the people who live there now or with their gods; do not allow them to stay. If they stay, they will cause you to sin against Me."

Discussion:

If your best friend commits a crime, and the judge asks you about it, what should you do?

What command/reminder did YHVH repeat?

What Feasts did YHVH command in this passage?

When the Israelites were allowed to enter the land, what were they to do?

Part V: Exodus 24:1-18

NT: Hebrews 9:19-30

Moses told the people all that YHVH commanded, and again they answered, "Yes, we will obey YHVH!" Moses wrote down everything YHVH had said.

Early the next morning, Moses built an altar at the base of the mountain. He set up twelve stone pillars: one for each tribe. He sent young Israelite men to offer burned offerings and sacrifices to YHVH. Moses collected the blood, and he splashed half of it against the altar. He put the other half in bowls. He read the Book of the Covenant to the people, and they said, "Yes, we will obey YHVH!"

Moses sprinkled the people with the blood from the sacrifices, and he said, "This is the blood of the covenant that YHVH has made with you."

Then Moses took with him Aaron, Aaron's sons Nadab and Abihu, and the seventy leaders; they went up the mountain as YHVH commanded. There they saw the God of Israel, and under His feet was a pavement of blue stones. God did not raise His hand to kill these men. They saw God, and they ate and drank.

YHVH said to Moses, "Come up to the mountain, and stay here. I will give you stone tablets with the Law I have written for you." Moses and Joshua headed up the mountain leaving Aaron and Hur in charge of the people.

When Moses went up the mountain, the cloud covered it. The glory of YHVH came down on top of Mount Sinai, and it covered the mountain for six days. On the seventh day, YHVH called to Moses from inside the cloud. From below in the Israelites' camp, the mountain looked like it was on fire. Moses walked into the cloud, and he stayed on the mountain for forty days and nights.

Discussion:

Who was allowed in the presence of God?

Why did Moses go back up the mountain after confirming YHVH's covenant with the Israelites?

Why is it important that they ate a meal in God's presence?

How long was Moses on the mountain?

Terumah (Contribution) – Exodus 25:1 - 27:19; I Kings 5:26 - 6:13

Portion:

Part I: Exodus 25:1-22

NT: II Corinthians 9:6-8

While Moses was on the mountain, YHVH said to him, "Tell the Israelites to bring Me an offering—if they are willing to give." God told Moses to receive gifts of gold, silver, and bronze as well as yarn dyed blue, purple, and bright red. He was also told to receive expensive linen, goat hair, ram skins dyed red, waterproof leather, acacia wood, olive oil, spices, and gemstones. They were going to build an amazing house! God Himself was going to live there in the middle of His people.

From acacia wood, YHVH commanded the people to build a box, like a treasure chest, also called an ark. He commanded that they build it forty-five inches long, twenty-seven inches wide, and twenty-seven inches high. They were commanded to cover the ark, inside and out, with pure gold. They were commanded to carry the ark by two gold-plated poles slid into four golden rings (two on each side). The poles were permanently to stay in the rings; they were not to be removed. The ark would hold the covenant Law that YHVH was writing on tablets of stone.

They were commanded to make a lid for the ark from pure, hammered gold. Two winged cherubim were to be hammered out of gold on the top of the atonement cover: one on each end, facing each other, with their wings spread to the sky. YHVH told Moses that He would meet with him there—between the two cherubim that sat over the Ark of the Covenant Law.

Discussion:

What is the Ark of the Covenant?

What was special about the lid to the Ark of the Covenant?

Where do we first find Cherubim in Scripture?

Part II: Exodus 25:23-40

NT: Hebrews 9:1-12

YHVH commanded the people to build a table from acacia wood. He told them to make it thirty-six inches long, eighteen inches wide, and twenty-seven inches high. They were to cover it in gold and make a wide rim of gold around the top. Like the ark, the table would also be carried by gold-plated poles. The table's pitchers, plates, and bowls were to be made of pure gold. The table was always to hold a special bread representing the Presence of God.

YHVH commanded the people to build a beautiful lampstand of pure, hammered gold. It was designed to look like a tree with three branches coming out of the main trunk on one side and three branches coming out of the main trunk on the other side. Each branch, including the center trunk, was to be decorated in hammered gold almond flowers and buds.

Seven lamps were to sit on the lampstand to give light to the area in front of the stand. The wick trimers and trays for the lampstand and lamps were also to be made of pure gold. All in all, seventy-five pounds of pure gold would be used to make the lampstand and lamps. Moses knew what these things should look like because YHVH showed him while he was on the mountain.

Discussion:

What was always to sit on top of the gold-plated table?

How many lamps was the lampstand made to hold?

Part III: Exodus 26:1-14

NT: Hebrews 8:1-6

YHVH commanded Moses and said, "Make a large tent, or a Tabernacle, out of ten pieces of fine linen cloth and blue, purple, and bright red yarn. Have a skilled artist sew pictures of cherubim onto the cloth. Each piece of cloth should be forty-two feet long and six feet wide. Sew five pieces of cloth together for one set and five pieces of cloth together for another set. Sew fifty loops of blue cloth onto the edge of each set. Be sure the loops on each set are lined up; then make fifty golden hooks to join the loops together. This will make the Tabernacle one piece.

Next, make another tent that will cover the Tabernacle. Make this tent from eleven pieces of goat hair cloth. These pieces must be forty-five feet long and six feet wide. Sew five pieces of cloth together for one set and the other six pieces together for a second set. Fold the sixth piece over the front of the Tabernacle. Sew fifty loops on the edge of the goat hair cloth, just as you did with the fine linen cloth, and join the loops with fifty bronze hooks. There will be eighteen inches hanging over the sides of the Tabernacle, so the goat hair cloth will protect the fine linen cloth.

Then make two more coverings for the Tabernacle: one from dyed red ram skins and the other from waterproof leather."

Discussion:

The first layer of curtains that YHVH instructed was very beautiful and sewn with pictures of cherubim. Could the people see these curtains?

Do you think that YHVH cared what His House looked like?

Do you think He cared more about the outside or the inside of His House? What can we learn from this?

Part IV: Exodus 26:15-37

NT: Matthew 27:50-52

YHVH commanded Moses: "Make the Tabernacle frame from acacia wood. Make each frame fifteen feet long and twenty-seven inches wide. Make twenty frames for the north side, twenty frames for the south side, six frames for the west side, and two frames for each corner of the east end of the Tabernacle. Each frame must have two silver bases to go under it.

Make crossbars of acacia wood to connect the Tabernacle frames. Make five crossbars to hold the frames together on one side and five crossbars to hold the frames together on the other side. Also make crossbars to hold the frames together on the west end. The crossbars should slide into golden rings. Cover the frames and the crossbars with gold. Be sure to make the Tabernacle the way I showed you on the mountain.

Make a curtain from fine linen and blue, purple, and bright red yarn. Have a skilled artist sew pictures of cherubim onto the curtain. Hang the curtain from golden hooks on four acacia wood posts. Cover the posts with gold, and set them in four silver bases. Place the Ark of the Covenant behind the curtain. This curtain will separate the Holy Place from the Most Holy Place. Put the table and the lampstand outside the curtain.

For the door of the Tabernacle, make a curtain from fine linen and blue, purple, and bright red yarn. Make golden hooks for the curtain, and hang it from five gold-covered acacia posts. Set the five posts in five bronze bases."

Discussion:

How long was the Tabernacle on the south and north sides?

Why was there a curtain on the inside of the Tabernacle?

Part V: Exodus 27:1-19

NT: Matthew 23:16-20

YHVH commanded Moses to build an altar for their burned offerings. He said, "Build it with acacia wood: four-and-a-half feet high and seven-and-a-half feet square. Make each of the corners stick out like a horn, and cover the entire altar with bronze.

Make all the altar tools with bronze: shovels, bowls, meat forks, and pans. Make a bronze screen to fit inside the altar, and put bronze rings on the four corners of the screen. Make bronze-covered acacia wood poles that slide through the rings when you carry the altar. Make the altar just as I've shown you on the mountain.

Make a wall of curtains to form a courtyard around the Tabernacle: one hundred and fifty feet on the north and south sides and seventy-five feet on the east and west sides. Use fine linen for the curtains, bronze for the posts and bases, and silver hooks to hold the curtains. Make a thirty-foot-wide curtain for the entry to the courtyard. Make it from fine linen and blue, purple, and bright red yarn. Everything used in the Tabernacle, as well as the tent pegs for the Tabernacle and courtyard, must be made of bronze."

Discussion:

YHVH's instructions are thorough. Still, how was Moses supposed to know *exactly* how to make the altar and other things for the Tabernacle?

Tetzaveh (You are to order) – Exodus 27:20 - 30:10; Ezekiel 43:10-27

Portion:

Part I: Exodus 27:20-28:14

NT: Matthew 25:1-13

YHVH continued to give Moses commands for the people. He said, "To keep the lampstand continually burning, have the people make clear oil of pressed olives. Aaron and his sons should keep the lamps burning.

Aaron and his sons will serve Me as priests. To set Aaron apart and to show him honor, make special clothes for him. For him and his sons, have skilled artists make a breastplate, an ephod, a robe, a tunic, a turban, and a sash. Make these things out of gold and fine linen with blue, purple, and bright red yarn.

Make the ephod this way: At the top corners of the ephod, or vest, there will be a pair of straps that tie over the priest's shoulders. At the bottom of the ephod will be a woven belt. Engrave the names of the sons of Israel on two onyx stones: six names on each stone. Mount one stone on one shoulder piece and the other stone on the other shoulder piece so that Aaron wears the names of Israel before YHVH. Mount the stones in gold settings, and attach braided gold chains to the settings."

Discussion:

How many special pieces of clothing were to be made for the priest?

What would the priest wear on his shoulders?

Were these expensive pieces of clothing?

Part II: Exodus 28:15-43

NT: Revelation 20:5-6

"The breastplate should be a nine-inch square folded double. Mount four rows of three precious stones on the front of the square. Mount the stones in gold. There will be twelve stones total: each stone engraved for one of the tribes of Israel. Fasten two gold rings to the top corner of the breastplate, and use gold ropes to attach the plate to the shoulder pieces of the ephod. Do the same to the bottom of the breastplate, and attach it to the waistband so that it doesn't swing when the priest walks. Whenever Aaron enters the Holy Place, he will wear the names of the children of Israel over his heart. Also put the Urim and the Thummim into the breastplate. These things will help Aaron in making decisions for the Israelites, and Aaron will always carry them when he is before YHVH.

Make the priest's outer robe from blue cloth with an opening for his head at the center and a collar woven around the opening to keep it from tearing. The hem of the robe should be decorated with golden bells and pomegranates made from blue, purple, and bright red yarn. The bells will ring when Aaron enters the Holy Place. This will keep him from being killed.

Engrave the words, 'Holy to YHVH' on a pure gold plate. Use a blue cord to fasten the plate to the front of Aaron's turban. Aaron will wear the plate on his forehead, and he will be blamed if anything is wrong with the Israelites' gifts. Aaron must always wear this plate so that YHVH will accept the people's gifts.

Make all the priests' tunics, turbans, and sashes out of fine linen. Sew designs onto the sashes. After these articles of clothing are made, put them on Aaron and his sons and anoint them as priests. Also make linen underclothes for the priests to wear when they enter the tent of meeting and when they come near the altar to serve as priests. If they do not wear these clothes, they will be guilty of doing wrong and will be killed. This law will last for Aaron and all his descendants."

Discussion:

Why would the sound of the bells keep Aaron from being killed?

How specific was YHVH about what the priests should wear?

Do you think YHVH cares about how his people approach Him?

Part III: Exodus 29:1-9

NT: Revelation 19:1-8

"This is what you will do when you anoint Aaron and his sons. You must do this before they can serve Me as priests: Take one young bull and two perfect rams. Make thick loaves of unleavened bread from fine flour and olive oil. Make thin loaves of unleavened bread brushed with olive oil. Put the loaves into a basket, and bring the basket, the bull, and the rams to the door of the tent of meeting. Bring Aaron and his sons to the door and wash them with water. Then dress Aaron in the clothing made for him, and anoint his head with a special anointing oil. Dress his sons in their tunics. Put turbans on their heads, and tie sashes around their waists. The priesthood is theirs."

Discussion:

Could Aaron and his sons serve in the Holy Place before they were anointed?

Part IV: Exodus 29:10-46

NT: Hebrews 10:11-23

"Bring the bull to the front of the tent of meeting. Aaron and his sons will put their hands on the bull's head. Kill the bull at the entrance to the tent. Put some of its blood on the horns of the altar, and pour the rest on the base. Take all the fat around the internal organs with the best part of the liver and the kidneys, and burn them on the altar. Burn the rest of the bull outside the camp because this is an offering for purification.

Next take one of the rams and have Aaron and his sons put their hands on its head as well. Kill it, and put its blood on the altar. Cut the ram into pieces, wash the internal organs, and burn the entire ram as a burned offering. The smell is pleasing to YHVH.

Take the second ram, and have Aaron and his sons put their hands on its head. Then kill the ram and put some of its blood on the priests' right ears, right thumbs, and the big toes of their right feet. Put the rest of the blood on the sides of the altar. Then take some of the blood from the altar, and mix it with the special anointing oil. Sprinkle this blood and oil on Aaron and his clothes and on his sons and their clothes.

Take the fat from the second lamb, the tail, the best part of the liver, the kidneys with the fat around them, and the right thigh. Give these things to the priests along with a thick and thin loaf from the breadbasket. The priests will wave this offering before YHVH. Then take these things, and burn them with the burned offering.

Take the breast of the ram, and wave it to YHVH; that will be your part to eat. The breast and the right thigh that was waved are the priests' food. Aaron and his sons will eat it with the bread from the basket. Any food left over should be burned. It is holy, and no one else may eat it.

It will take seven days to ordain the priests, and every day a bull will be sacrificed. After that, the altar will be holy. Then two lambs will be sacrificed daily: one in the morning and the other in the early evening. Both lambs will be sacrificed with an offering of fine flour and oil and a drink offering of wine. These offerings should be made every day. I will come to the tent, and I will meet with you there. I will live in the middle of the camp. The people will know that I am YHVH who brought them out of Egypt so that I could live with them."

Discussion:

How long did God say it would take to consecrate the priests and the altar?

What parts of the animal were always offered to YHVH?

After the time of consecration, what sacrifice was to be made daily?

Part V: Exodus 30:1-10

NT: Revelation 8:1-5; Philippians 4:10-20

"Build an incense altar from acacia wood. The altar should be eighteen inches square and three feet high. Cover it and its horns with pure gold. Make gold rings to hold the gold-covered poles which are used to carry the altar. Put the altar outside the curtain that hides the Ark of the Covenant.

Every morning Aaron will burn incense, and every evening he will burn it again. Nothing else may be burned on this altar except the required incense. Once a year, Aaron will cleanse the altar by putting blood from a yearly offering on the altar's horns. The altar belongs to YHVH."

Discussion:

Was the altar of incense an altar for sacrifices?

What was to happen differently once a year?

Ki Tisa (When you take) –
Exodus 30:11 - 34:35; I Kings 18:1-39

Portion:

Part I: Exodus 30:11-38

NT: Luke 1:5-23

YHVH continued to give Moses His laws for the people. He said, "When you count the Israelites in a census, every man who is over twenty years old must pay a half-shekel ransom to buy back his life from YHVH. The money will be used to buy things needed in the tent of meeting. This payment will remind YHVH that the Israelites have been bought back.

Make a bronze bowl that will be used for washing. Put the bowl full of water between the Tabernacle and the altar. So that they will not die, Aaron and his sons will wash their hands and feet before entering the tent and before offering a sacrifice to YHVH.

Take twelve pounds of myrrh, twelve pounds of cassia, and half as much cinnamon and cane. Mix these spices with a gallon of olive oil. Use this special oil to anoint the tent of meeting and everything in it. Also use this oil to anoint Aaron and his sons, but do not use it on anyone else or for any other purpose. It is holy. Whoever makes an oil like it will be cut off from the people of Israel.

Use equal amounts of gum resin, onycha, galbanum, and frankincense. Make a holy incense to burn in front of the Ark of the Covenant on the altar of incense. Do not make incense like it for any other purpose. It is holy."

Discussion:

Why did Aaron and his sons have to wash in the bronze bowl?

Could the priests be anointed with regular oil?

Name one ingredient in the holy anointing oil?

Name one ingredient in the holy incense?

Both these things were called holy. What does this mean?

Part II: Exodus 31:1-18

NT: I Corinthians 12:20-25

"I have chosen Bezalel from the tribe of Judah. I have given him the wisdom to work with metals, wood, and precious stones. I have picked Oholiab from the tribe of Dan to help him. I have also chosen other artists, and I have given them the skills they need to make everything I have required. Make everything exactly as I have commanded."

Then YHVH said to Moses, "Tell the Israelites that they must obey all of My Sabbath rules. Sabbath is our sign so you will remember that YHVH has set you apart. Anyone who blasphemes the Sabbath must be killed; anyone who does any work on the Sabbath must be cut off from Israel. YHVH made the heavens and the earth in six days, and then He rested on the seventh day."

When YHVH had finished speaking, He gave Moses two tablets of stone. On those stones, the very finger of God had written down the laws of the covenant.

Discussion:

Why is it so important that YHVH's people keep the Sabbath?

Part III: Exodus 32:1-35

NT: Acts 19:26-28

When the people saw that Moses had been on the mountain a long time, they became worried. "Aaron," they said, "make us mighty ones who will lead us. We do not know what has happened to Moses."

Aaron listened to the people. He told them to bring him their jewelry so that he could use it to make an image. He melted the gold, and he formed it to the shape of a calf. The people cried out, "Israel, this is your god who brought you out of Egypt."

When Aaron saw the people's reaction, he built an altar in front of the calf. He said, "Tomorrow we will have a feast to YHVH!" The people woke up early to eat, drink, offer sacrifices, and have a huge party.

YHVH said to Moses, "Go down to the people you brought from Egypt. They have already sinned against Me! They have made an idol in the shape of a calf. They have burned offerings to it and said, 'Israel, look who brought you out of Egypt!' Stand back, Moses, so that I can destroy the people and rebuild My nation through you."

Moses begged God. He said, "YHVH, do not do this thing! Our enemies will think that You rescued your people just to destroy them in the wilderness! Remember Abraham, Isaac, and Jacob! Save the people for *their* sake." YHVH listened to Moses, and He did not destroy the people.

Moses went down the mountain carrying the two tablets of stone. On the tablets, front and back, YHVH had carved the words of His covenant Law. When Joshua heard the people below, he said to Moses, "It sounds like war!" Moses answered, "No, it sounds like singing."

When Moses came to the camp, he saw the people dancing around a golden image. He was angry. He threw down the tablets that YHVH had made—smashing them to pieces on the ground. Then Moses burned the golden calf in the fire. He ground the ashes into a powder, and he put it in the Israelites' water so that they would drink it.

Moses asked Aaron, "How did the people talk you into doing this terrible thing?"

Aaron answered and said, "You know how these people are always ready to sin. They wanted a god who would speak to YHVH and lead them, so I asked them to bring me their jewelry. I threw the gold into the fire, and it turned into this calf!"

Moses stood at the entrance of the camp, and he called out in a loud voice, "Whoever is on YHVH's side, come here!" The Levites ran to Moses. Then Moses said to the Levites, "Grab a sword, and kill your brothers, friends, and neighbors." The Levites obeyed, and they killed about three-thousand people; they were blessed for choosing God over their friends and family. YHVH set them apart from the rest of the Israelites.

The next day Moses talked to the people. He said, "You have done very wrong. But I will talk to YHVH and see if He will forgive you." So Moses went to back to YHVH.

"They have sinned a huge sin, God," Moses said. "But please forgive them! If You will not forgive them, erase my name from Your book too."

YHVH answered and said, "I will only erase those who have sinned. Lead the people to the place I told you about. My angel will go in front of you. However, I *will* punish them for their sin."

YHVH brought a plague to the Israelites because of the golden calf.

Discussion:

What did the people think had happened to Moses?

What did the people think they needed in place of Moses?

What did Aaron make for them?

Were they having a feast to a false god?

Did YHVH think they were worshipping Him?

What did Moses do when he saw the people's sin?

Part IV: Exodus 33:1-23

NT: Romans 9:14-16

YHVH said to Moses, "Take the people to the land I promised to Abraham, Isaac, and Jacob. I will send an angel ahead of you to drive out your enemies, but I will not go with you. The people are so stubborn that if I went with you I might destroy you along the way. Tell the people to take off their jewelry, and I will decide what to do with you."

When the people heard what YHVH had said, they cried. No one put on any jewelry.

Moses set up a tent outside the camp. He called it the tent of meeting. When someone needed to ask YHVH a question, they went to that tent. When Moses went to the tent, the pillar of cloud came down and covered the doorway of the tent. Whenever the Israelites saw that Moses was in the tent of meeting, they each worshipped YHVH at the doorway of their own tents. YHVH spoke to Moses the way a man speaks with his friend. Moses went back and forth between the camp and the tent of meeting, but Joshua stayed at the tent.

Moses said to YHVH, "You tell me to lead these people, but who will go with me? If You are pleased with me, teach me Your ways so that I can continue to please You. Remember, this nation is Yours."

YHVH replied, "My Presence will go with you and give you rest."

Moses answered, "If Your Presence does not go with us, do not send us. How will anyone know that we are Yours if You are not with us? We will be like every other people on Earth."

YHVH said, "I am pleased with you; I will do as you've asked."

Then Moses pleaded, "YHVH, show me Your glory!"

YHVH answered, "I will cause all My goodness to pass in front of you, and I will speak My name: YHVH. I will have mercy on whomever I wish to have mercy, and I will have compassion on whomever I wish to have compassion. But you cannot see My face and live. Therefore, I will hide you in a place in the rock, and I will cover you with My hand until I have passed by. You will see My back."

Discussion:

Because of YHVH's anger over Israel's sin with the golden calf, what did He say would happen?

Did YHVH agree to go with the people?

Part V: Exodus 34:1-35

NT: II Corinthians 3:7-18

YHVH said to Moses, "Cut two more tablets of stone. I will write the same words on them that I wrote on the first two stones which you broke." So Moses did, and then he headed up the mountain with the tablets.

As God had promised, His presence passed before Moses saying "YHVH, YHVH, the compassionate and gracious God, slow to anger, full of love and faithfulness, loving thousands and forgiving sin. The guilty, however, He punishes to the third and fourth generation."

Moses bowed low and worshiped. He said, "YHVH, if You are happy with me, please go with us. This is a stubborn people, but forgive our sin. Take us as your own treasure." Then YHVH said, "I am making a covenant with you. I will do mighty things like no one has ever seen. Everyone around you will see that YHVH is with you. Obey what I tell you to do. I will go ahead of you and drive your enemies from the land. Be careful not to make covenants with other nations. Do not worship any other god, for I am a jealous God.

Do not make idols.

Celebrate the Feast of Unleavened Bread.

Redeem the first-born of your livestock and your first-born sons. They will not be allowed before Me without a ransom.

Keep My Sabbaths.

Celebrate the Feast of Weeks (Shavuot).

If your men come before YHVH three times a year, I will give you more and more land. Your enemies will not try to take it from you while your men are away for the Feasts.

Do not offer My blood sacrifices with anything containing yeast, and do not keep any leftovers from the Passover sacrifice. It must be gone before the next morning.

Bring me the best of your first fruits.

Do not cook a goat in his mother's milk."

Moses was on the mountain for forty days without eating food or drinking water. He wrote down the words that YHVH commanded him to write. When he was finished, he came down the mountain with the tablets of the covenant. His face glowed from the presence of YHVH, and the people were afraid of him. After Moses spoke YHVH's words to the people, he covered his face with a veil. When he went into the tent to speak with YHVH, he removed his veil; when he came out to speak with the people, he covered his face again.

Discussion:

Why did YHVH repeat the commands to the people?

Vayak'hel (He assembled) –
Exodus 35:1 - 38:20; I Kings 7:40-50;
II Kings 12:1-17

Pekudei (Accounts) –
Exodus 38:21 - 40:38; I Kings 7:40 - 8:21

(In leap years these portions are read separately.)

Portion:

Part I: Exodus 35:1-36:38

NT: II Corinthians 8-9

Moses gathered the people and said, "These are YHVH's instructions: For six days you should be working, but do not do any work on the seventh day. The Sabbath is set apart for YHVH. Whoever works on that day will be killed. Do not light a fire on the Sabbath."

Then just as God had commanded, Moses asked the people to bring an offering. He told them what YHVH had requested, and the people were happy to give. They brought gold, silver, bronze, blue yarn, purple yarn, bright red yarn, fine linen, goat hair, ram skins, leather, acacia wood, olive oil, spices, and precious stones. Skilled artists and builders came to build the tent and coverings, the hooks, the frames, the crossbars, the posts, the bases, and everything needed for the Tabernacle.

Bezalel, Oholiab, and other Israelite artists and builders began to build everything exactly as YHVH had said. The people brought their offerings, and the artists worked. This continued for days and days until the builders told Moses that they had more than enough materials. The people wanted to continue giving, but Moses told them to stop.

The Israelites made the curtains for the Tabernacle out of fine linen. There were pictures of cherubim sewn into them in blue, purple, and bright red yarn. They connected the curtains with golden hooks. They made three tents to cover the holy tent with goat hair, ram skins, and leather. They made bronze hooks for these tents. They made the gold-covered frames from acacia wood, and they set them into silver bases. They made the gold-covered crossbars from acacia wood, and they slid them into golden rings. They made a fine linen curtain for the inside of the Tabernacle, and they made a fine linen curtain for the door of the tent. These curtains were beautifully embroidered with blue, purple, and bright red yarn. They made them exactly as YHVH told Moses.

Discussion:

Why did Moses remind the people of the Sabbath laws before they began to build?

Why did Moses tell the people to stop bringing offerings?

Were the people happy to build the Tabernacle?

Part II (Exodus 37:1-29):

NT: Revelation 11:1-13, 15:5-8

Bezalel made the ark from acacia wood. He covered it inside and out with gold. He made four gold rings, and he attached them to the bottom of the ark. He attached two rings on one side and two rings on the other side. He made gold-covered poles, and he slid them into the rings. He made it exactly as YHVH had commanded.

He made a pure gold lid to cover the ark. Out of the same piece of solid gold, he hammered two cherubim. He made one cherub on one end and another cherub on the other end, and he made them facing each other.

He made the table from acacia wood. He covered the table in gold, and he slid four gold-plated poles into four golden rings. From pure gold, he made all the things needed for the table: plates, bowls, cups, and the pitchers used for pouring the drink offerings.

He made the lampstand from one piece of hammered gold. He hammered three branches on one side of the center and three branches on the other side. Each branch had three almond-flower shaped cups. The center branch of the lampstand had four cups. He made seven gold lamps for the lampstand. Everything needed for the lampstand he made from solid gold—just as YHVH had said.

He made the altar for burning incense. He covered the acacia wood altar with gold. He made the gold-covered rings to hold the gold-covered poles that were used to carry the altar. Then he made the special anointing oil and the holy incense exactly as YHVH said.

Discussion:

Who is the man YHVH gifted to make/oversee the Tabernacle and its furnishings?

Part III: Exodus 38:1-31

NT: Hebrews 9:1-12

He made the altar for burned offerings. He covered the acacia wood altar in bronze. He used bronze to make the pots, the shovels, the meat forks, the sprinkling bowls, and the firepans. He made a bronze screen to fit halfway inside the altar. He made bronze rings and the four bronze-covered poles that were used to carry the altar.

He made a bronze bowl and stand for washing.

He made a large courtyard around the outside of the Tabernacle. He made the courtyard from fine linen curtains, acacia wood posts, bronze bases, and silver hooks. The curtain for the doorway was made of fine linen sewn with blue, purple, and bright red yarn. The curtain was thirty feet long and seven-and-a-half feet high, which was the same height as the rest of the curtains around the courtyard.

Bezalel was in charge of making everything needed for the Tabernacle. Oholiab was an expert in sewing and engraving, and he helped Bezalel with the work. All in all, in the building of the Tabernacle they used over 2,000 pounds of gold, 7,550 pounds of silver, and 5,000 pounds of bronze.

Discussion:

How would you describe the instructions of YHVH regarding the building of the Tabernacle?

Who helped Bezalel in building the Tabernacle?

Part IV: Exodus 39:1-43

NT: Hebrews 9:13-28

    They made Aaron's clothes, just as YHVH had commanded, out of blue, purple, and bright red yarn sewn into fine linen. They made a vest, called an ephod, from fine linen and gold with blue, purple, and red yarn. First, they hammered the gold into sheets, and then they cut the gold into thin strips that they wove with the yarn. They attached shoulder straps to the top corners of the ephod, and they wove a belt along the bottom. They wrote the names of six tribes of Israel on one onyx stone and the other six tribes on another. Then they put the stones into gold settings, and they attached them to the shoulders of the ephod.

    They made the breastplate like the ephod from fine linen and gold with blue, purple, and bright red yarn. They made it as a nine-inch square folded in half to make a pocket. They set four rows of three beautiful jewels into the front it. The names of the sons of Israel were carefully carved into the jewels: one name per jewel.

They made two gold rings for the upper corners of the breastplate. They twisted gold into chains, and they put the chains into the rings. They used the chains to attach the breastplate to the ephod. Then they made two more gold rings for the bottom of the breastplate, and they used blue yarn to attach the breastplate to the belt.

They made the priest's outer robe from blue cloth. They made pomegranates from yarn and bells from pure gold, and they attached them to the hem of the robe.

They sewed inner robes made of fine linen for Aaron and his sons. They also made Aaron's turban and all the priests' underclothes and caps of fine linen. They made linen sashes for the robes, and they used blue, purple, and bright red yarn to sew designs into the cloth.

They cut a plate of pure gold that they attached to the front of Aaron's turban. Into the gold they carved the words, "Holy to YHVH."

When the Israelites had finished making every piece needed to build the Tabernacle, they brought everything to Moses for inspection. When Moses saw that everything had been made perfectly according to God's instruction, he blessed the people for their hard work.

Discussion:

Can you name some of the pieces that Moses would have inspected that day? (Use Exodus 39:32-41 for reference.)

Part V: Exodus 40:1-38

NT: I Corinthians 3:16-17

On the first day of the first month, in the second year after leaving Egypt, YHVH told Moses to set up the Tabernacle. Moses placed the Ark of the Covenant behind the curtain as commanded by YHVH. In front of the curtain, he set up the table and all its plates and bowls, the lampstand and its lamps, and the altar of incense. He placed the bronze altar in front of the Tabernacle entrance, and he put the bowl for washing between the altar and the Tabernacle. All around the Tabernacle, he set up the courtyard.

Once everything had been put into place, the entire Tabernacle and all its furnishings were anointed with the holy oil. Then Aaron and his sons were brought to the entrance of the tent. They were washed, anointed with oil, and dressed in their holy clothing. Aaron's sons were anointed as well because they would serve as priests after their father. The priesthood was given to Aaron and his sons.

When everything had been done exactly as YHVH said, the cloud came and covered the tent. The glory of YHVH filled the Tabernacle. In all the Israelites' travels through the wilderness, they followed the cloud. If the cloud lifted, they moved. If the cloud did not lift, they stayed where they were.

Discussion:

Who was required to set up and anoint the Tabernacle for the first time?

What happened when everything was built, set-up, and anointed according to God's instructions?

Vayikra (He called) –
Leviticus 1:1 - 5:26; Is. 43:21 - 44:23; I Samuel 15:2-34

Portion:

Part I: Leviticus 1:1-17

NT: Romans 15:15-17

YHVH called to Moses from the Tabernacle, and He taught him the rules for offering sacrifices to YHVH. He said, "If you offer a burned offering to YHVH, it should be a perfect male from your flock or herd. If the animal is a cow from your herd, it will be accepted by YHVH if you place your hand on the animal's head and sacrifice it at the Tabernacle entrance. If the animal is a sheep or goat from your flock, the person offering the animal must kill it on the north side of the altar. Aaron's sons, the priests, will sprinkle the animal's blood on the altar. After you have cut the animal into pieces and washed the organs and legs, the priest will put the pieces on the altar. This burned offering is a sweet smell to YHVH.

If you are offering a bird to YHVH, you will offer a turtledove or a young pigeon. The priest will kill the bird over the altar and then drain its blood on the side of the altar. The priest will pluck the feathers and throw them on the east side of the altar. Then he will burn the bird on the altar. This is a sweet smell to YHVH."

Discussion:

What is the difference between offering an animal from the herd and an animal from the flock?

What do all the sacrificial animals have in common? What kind of offering does YHVH accept?

Part II: Leviticus 2:1-16

NT: Acts 24:1-19

"When you bring a grain offering to YHVH, bring fine flour, olive oil, and frankincense to the priest. The priest will take a handful of the offering and burn it to YHVH. The rest of the offering belongs to Aaron and his sons, the priests.

When you bring a grain offering that is cooked, bring it this way: Bake fine flour and olive oil without yeast, or cook fine flour and oil like a pancake. The priest will burn a portion of the offering to YHVH; the rest will belong to Aaron and his sons.

When you bring a grain offering to YHVH, do not bring anything made with yeast or honey. You may bring first fruits offerings made with yeast and honey, but you may not burn them as a sweet smell to YHVH. Also, do not forget to put salt in all your grain offerings, as salt is a sign of our covenant.

If you bring a first fruits grain offering, crush the heads of grain and roast them in fire. Pour incense and oil over it, and then give it to the priest. He will burn some of it to YHVH."

Discussion:

What was a food/grain offering not to be offered with? What was it to be offered with?

Part III: Leviticus 3:1-17

NT: II Timothy 2:15; Hebrews 5

"If you are bringing a fellowship offering, bring a perfect male or female animal from your herd or flock. Put your hand on the animal's head, and kill it at the entrance of the Tabernacle. Then Aaron's sons will splash the animal's blood against the altar.

Give the fat, the internal organs with the fat connected to them, the kidneys, and the best part of the liver to the priest. He will burn them as an offering to YHVH.

If you are offering a sheep, also offer the entire fat tail. This is a law for all your generations: do not eat the fat or the blood."

Discussion:

What part(s) of the sacrifice belonged to YHVH?

Part IV: Leviticus 4:1-35

NT: Romans 8:1-13

YHVH said to Moses, "This is what you need to do if an Israelite realizes they have accidentally disobeyed YHVH's commands. These are the rules if it is the anointed priest who disobeys or if the whole congregation of Israel is guilty of disobedience: When they realize they have sinned, they will bring a perfect young bull to the Tabernacle door. If the priest has sinned, he will place his hand on the animal's head before killing it. If the congregation has sinned, the elders will place their hands on the animal's head before killing it. Then the priest will dip his finger in the animal's blood and sprinkle it seven times before YHVH in front of the sanctuary curtain. The priest will also put some of the animal's blood on the horns of the altar of incense. He will pour the rest of the blood at the base of the altar for burned offerings. The fat and organs will be removed and burned just like with the fellowship offering. The rest of the animal will be burned outside the camp in the place where the ashes are thrown.

When a leader sins, he will bring a perfect male goat as a purification offering. When another member of the congregation sins, they will bring a perfect female goat as a purification offering. The offeror will put their hands on the animal's head and kill it at the north side of the altar. The priest will put some of the blood on the horns of the incense altar and pour the rest at the base of the altar. The fat will be burned just like with the other offerings. The priest will make atonement for the person offering the sacrifice, and that person will be forgiven. The smell of these offerings is pleasing to YHVH."

Discussion:

What kind of goat/sheep, male or female, was to be offered if a leader sinned?

What kind of goat/sheep, male or female, was to be offered if a non-leader sinned?

Part V: Leviticus 5:1-19

NT: Hebrews 10:1-14; 13:11-16

"If anyone sees or hears something wrong and does not speak up when the judge asks them to, they are guilty. They are responsible for the sin.

If anyone realizes that they are guilty of touching the dead body of an unclean animal, or if they realize they have touched something else that has made them unclean, or if they realize that they promised to do something they should not have promised to do, they must confess their sin. Then the guilty person must bring a female goat or lamb as a purification offering. The priest will make things right between them and God.

If the guilty person cannot afford a lamb or a goat, they may bring two turtledoves or pigeons instead: one as a burned offering and one as a purification offering. If they cannot afford the birds, they may bring three-and-a-half pounds of fine flour. The flour must be offered without olive oil or incense because it is a purification offering. The priest will burn a portion to YHVH, and the guilty person will be forgiven."

YHVH said to Moses, "Someone might accidentally do something to harm one of YHVH's holy things. That person must bring a perfect ram as a guilt offering. It must be worth the right amount of silver because the guilty person is paying for what he did wrong. He must also pay one-fifth of what the holy thing is worth, and he must give the money to the priest. YHVH will forgive him.

Someone might accidentally do something that YHVH has commanded against. That person is guilty. They must bring a perfect ram that is worth the right amount of money. They were guilty, but YHVH will forgive them."

Discussion:

If someone cannot afford their purification offering, what can they bring?

Tzav (Give an order) –
Leviticus 6:1 - 8:36; Jeremiah 7:21 - 8:3, 9:22-23

Portion:

Part I: Leviticus 6:1-13

NT: Matthew 3:7-12

YHVH said to Moses, "An Israelite might sin by tricking his neighbor. He might steal by keeping something that he was given to watch over or by finding a lost thing and keeping it. He might cheat his neighbor or lie about sinning. Once he has repented of his sin, he should pay back everything he has taken plus one-fifth more and bring a guilt offering to the priest for YHVH. Then he will be forgiven.

The priests must leave the burned offerings on the altar all night, and the fire must not be allowed to go out. Every morning, the priest will add new firewood and place the offerings on it. Before removing the ashes of the burned offerings, the priest will put on his linen clothes and linen underclothes. Then he will change his clothes and take the ashes to a clean place outside the camp."

Discussion:

If someone is guilty of keeping someone's property, how much do they need to pay back?

How long was the fire of the altar to stay burning?

Part II: Leviticus 6:14-30

NT: Matthew 16:5-12

"When a grain offering is brought to YHVH, the priest will burn a portion of it for YHVH. The rest of the grain offering belongs to Aaron and his sons. It must not be eaten with yeast, and it must be eaten in the courtyard of the Tabernacle.

When a son of Aaron is anointed priest, he must bring a grain offering to YHVH. He must bring three-and-a-half pounds of fine flour: half in the morning and half in the evening. The offering must be cooked with oil like a pancake and served to YHVH in broken pieces. Every bit of it should be burned. The priest's offerings to YHVH may not be eaten.

The purification offering should be killed before YHVH in the same place as the burned offering. The priest who sacrifices the purification offering will be the one to eat it. Everything that touches the meat becomes holy. If the meat is cooked in a clay pot, the pot must be destroyed. If the meat is cooked in a bronze pot, the pot must be carefully cleaned. Any of the priest's sons may eat the sacrifice unless its blood was taken into the Holy Place. In that case, the sacrifice must be burned and not eaten."

Discussion:

Who could eat the meat of a purification offering?

If the meat was cooked in a clay pot, what should be done to the pot? Why?

Part III: Leviticus 7:1-21

NT: I Corinthians 10:20-31

"The holy guilt offering must be killed where the burned offering is killed. Its blood must be sprinkled on the sides of the altar. The fat tail, all the fat surrounding the organs, the kidneys, and the best part of the liver must be burned to YHVH. The same rules apply for the purification offering. Any male in a priest's family may eat the rest of the guilt and purification offerings as long as they eat it in the set-apart place. The priest may also keep the skin of the animal. Every grain offering belongs to the priest who offered it to YHVH.

Anyone may offer a fellowship offering to YHVH. If the offering is being sacrificed because of thankfulness to YHVH, the Israelite who is bringing the offering should also bring thick unleavened loaves of bread made with olive oil, thin unleavened loaves brushed with oil, and thick loaves of fine flour and olive oil. He should also bring thick loaves of leavened bread. He should give one of each kind of loaf to the priest who sprinkled the animal's blood against the altar. The meat of a thankfulness offering must be eaten that same day. The meat of a vow or freewill offering may be eaten the next day, but after that any leftover meat must be burned. Anyone who eats it will be guilty.

If the meat touches something unclean, it must be burned and not eaten. If a person who has become unclean eats the meat of a fellowship offering, he must be cut off from his people."

Discussion:

Are the loaves of a fellowship offering burned to YHVH? Why?

Who eats the meat of a thankfulness, vow, or freewill offering?

Who eats the meat of a guilt or purification offering?

Part IV: Leviticus 7:22-38

NT: I John 1

"Do not eat the internal fat of any sacrificial animal. If you find the animal already dead, you may use the fat for some other purpose. Don't eat it. Blood also must never be eaten.

When an Israelite brings a fellowship offering, they must sacrifice the fat to YHVH. They must bring the breast with the fat and wave the breast to YHVH. Then the priest will burn the fat to YHVH, but the breast will belong to the priest. The right thigh should also be given to the priest. The right thigh and the breast belong to the priests as their share of the offerings."

These are the rules for sacrifices that YHVH gave to Moses.

Discussion:

Which animals are the sacrificial animals?

Part V: Leviticus 8:1-36

NT: Mark 11:17-19

This is what happened on the day the priests were anointed: YHVH said to Moses, "Bring Aaron and his sons and their clothes. Bring the special anointing oil, the bull for the purification offering, two rams, and a basket of unleavened bread. Then call the people to the Tabernacle door."

As the people watched, Moses washed Aaron and his sons with water. He dressed Aaron in all his priestly clothes, and he put the Urim and the Thummim in the breastplate.

Moses anointed the Tabernacle and everything in it. He sprinkled the altar seven times, and he anointed Aaron's head with the special oil. Then Moses dressed Aaron's sons in their robes, belts, and caps.

Next, Moses brought the bull for the purification offering. Aaron and his sons put their hands on the bull's head, and Moses killed the bull. With his finger, Moses put some of the blood on the corners of the altar of incense. Then he poured the rest of the blood at the base of the altar. Moses took the kidneys, the best part of the liver, and all the fat around the organs. He burned them to YHVH. He took the rest of the bull and burned it outside the camp.

Moses brought the first ram, and Aaron and his sons put their hands on its head. Moses killed it, and he sprinkled the blood on the sides of the altar. Moses cut the ram into pieces. He washed the organs and legs, and then he burned the whole ram on the altar. It was a burned offering, and its smell was pleasing to YHVH.

Moses brought the other ram, and Aaron and his sons put their hands on its head. Moses killed it, and he put some of its blood on the priests' right earlobes, right thumbs, and the big toes of their right feet.

Moses sprinkled blood on the sides of the altar. Then he took a loaf of unleavened bread from the basket, and he put it in the priest's hands along with the fat, kidneys, liver, and right thigh. The priest waved the things to YHVH; then Moses burned them as a pleasing smell to YHVH. Moses took the breast and waved it to YHVH as an offering. The breast belonged to Moses.

Moses mixed the blood from the altar with some of the special oil. With the mixture, he sprinkled Aaron and his sons and their clothing. He did this to set them apart for YHVH.

Then Moses said to Aaron, "You and your sons will eat the meat from the sacrifices. Cook it at the entrance of the tent, and eat it with the bread from the basket. Stay at the Tabernacle for seven days. That is how long it will take to ordain you as priests."

Discussion:

What part(s) of the animal should never be eaten?

What did the priests wave before the Lord when they were being ordained?

Sh'mini (Eighth) –
Leviticus 9:1 - 11:47; II Samuel 6:1 - 7:17; Ezekiel 36:16-38

Portion:

Part I: Leviticus 9:1-24

NT: Hebrews 12:25-29

On the eighth day, after the priests had been ordained, Moses called Aaron and his sons and the elders of Israel. He told Aaron to offer a purification offering and a burned offering. Then Moses told Aaron what to say to the Israelites. He said, "Take a male goat for a purification offering, a perfect one-year-old calf and lamb for a burned offering, and an ox and a ram for a fellowship offering. Sacrifice them with a grain offering. YHVH will show Himself today."

Aaron sacrificed his purification and burned offerings to make things right between him and YHVH, and he sacrificed the people's offerings to make things right between them and YHVH. He offered both sacrifices exactly as he had been commanded. In addition to these sacrifices, Aaron also performed the morning's burned offering.

When the offerings were finished, Aaron lifted his hands to bless the people. Then Moses and Aaron went into the Tabernacle. When they came out, they blessed the people together. Then the glory of YHVH appeared to the people. Fire from the presence of YHVH completely consumed the burned offering and the fat from the sacrifices. When the people saw the glory, they fell on their faces and shouted for joy!

Discussion:

Why were the people so happy to see the fire consume the sacrifices?

Part II: Leviticus 10:1-11

NT: II Corinthians 6:14-7:1

Two of Aaron's sons, Nadab and Abihu, offered incense to YHVH that He had not allowed them to bring. Fire came from the presence of YHVH and killed the two men instantly. Moses said to Aaron, "This is what God meant when He said that He would prove His holiness in front of all the people." Aaron said nothing.

Moses called two of Aaron's nephews, and he told them to carry their cousins' bodies outside the camp. Then Moses told Aaron and his living sons, Eleazar and Ithamar, not to mourn. He said, "The rest of us will mourn for those YHVH has destroyed, but you may not. Do not tear your clothes or uncover your heads, or you will die. Do not leave the Tabernacle, because you have been anointed."

Then YHVH spoke to Aaron. He said, "You and your sons must not drink wine before serving in the Tabernacle. This is so you can judge between what is holy and what is not and teach the Israelites the difference."

Discussion:

What had Aaron's sons done wrong?

Why do you think YHVH spoke to Aaron about wine in the Tabernacle after the death of his sons?

Part III: Leviticus 10:12-20

NT: I Peter 1:22-23

Moses reminded Aaron and his sons about the food left over from the offerings. The leftovers from the grain offering belonged to Aaron and his sons. He told them to eat it beside the altar because it was very holy. The waved breast and the presented thigh belonged to the priests and to their sons and daughters. They were commanded to eat the meat in a clean place.

Moses asked Aaron what they had done with the goat from the purification offering. He asked why it had been burned and not eaten in the set apart place as YHVH commanded. Aaron told Moses that because of what had just happened he didn't feel he could eat it with the right attitude. Moses accepted this explanation.

Discussion:

Why was Moses checking to make sure everything was done perfectly?

Why was Moses upset when he saw that the purification offering had not been eaten but burned?

Part IV: Leviticus 11:1-23

NT: Mark 7:1-20

YHVH spoke to Moses and Aaron. He told them about the clean animals He created for food. He said, "Animals that chew the cud and have a divided hoof are to be eaten. Animals that only have a divided hoof or only chew the cud are unclean and are not to be eaten. The dead bodies of unclean animals must not even be touched.

In the water, creatures with fins and scales are to be eaten. Fish that only have fins or only have scales are not to be eaten. The dead bodies of unclean fish and water animals should not even be touched.

Birds of prey such as the eagle, the vulture, the kite, the raven, the hawk, the gull, the cormorant, the stork, the osprey, and the owl are not to be eaten.

You may not eat flying insects that walk on all fours unless they have jointed legs for hopping on the ground: The locust, the cricket, and the grasshopper are for food. All other insects and creeping things, flying or crawling, are unclean."

Discussion:

What kind of fish may be eaten?

What kind of four-footed animals may be eaten?

May a worm be eaten? Why?

May an eagle be eaten? Why?

Part V: Leviticus 11:24-47

NT: Acts 10:9-22; I Peter 1:14-16

"If you touch the dead bodies of any of these unclean things, you will be unclean until evening. If you pick up the dead bodies of any of these unclean things, you must wash your clothes. You will be unclean until evening.

All reptiles and rodents are unclean.

If an unclean animal dies, the thing it falls on will become unclean too. The unclean thing must be washed with water, and it will be unclean until evening. Then it will become clean *unless* it is made from clay. You must destroy the thing made of clay. If water from an unclean pot is spilled or splashed on any food, that food becomes unclean too.

A spring or well will stay clean even if an unclean thing falls into it.

If an unclean animal dies on seeds you are going to plant, you may still use them. If you have already watered the seeds before the animal dies on them, they are unclean. You must not plant them.

Just like with the unclean animals, you will also be unclean until evening if you touch the dead bodies of clean animals.

Do not make yourself unclean by eating any unclean animal. I am YHVH who brought you out of Egypt to be your God. Be holy because I am holy."

Discussion:

Why could most things be washed with water while a clay thing had to be destroyed?

If someone touched the dead body of a clean animal, would they still be clean?

Tazria (She conceives) –
Leviticus 12:1 - 13:59; II Kings 4:42 - 5:19;
Ezekiel 45:18 - 46:15; Isaiah 66:1, 23-24

Metzora (Person afflicted with tzara'at) –
Leviticus 14:1 - 15:33; II Kings 7:3-20;
Malachi 3:4-24

(In leap years these portions are read separately.)

Portion:

Part I: Leviticus 12:1-8

NT: Luke 2:6-40

YHVH said to Moses, "After a woman gives birth to a son, she is unclean for seven days. She must have her son circumcised on the eighth day. Then, after thirty-three more days, she must go to the Tabernacle to be purified. She must not touch anything holy until she is purified. If a woman gives birth to a daughter, she is unclean for two weeks; she must wait sixty-six more days to be purified. When it is time for her purification, she will bring a one-year-old lamb for a burned offering and a pigeon or a dove for a purification offering. If she cannot afford to bring a lamb, she may bring two doves or pigeons instead of the lamb and the bird. After the sacrifice is complete, she will be clean."

Discussion:

What day is a baby boy to be circumcised?

What sacrifice was to be brought as a purification offering after childbirth?

Part II: Leviticus 13:1-46

NT: Luke 17:11-18

YHVH said to Moses and Aaron, "When anyone has swelling, or a rash, or their skin looks shiny and strange in some way, they should be examined by a priest. If the unusual spot seems to affect more than the top of the skin, if the hair on the spot has turned white, or if there is raw flesh in the swelling, the priest will decide that the spot is contagious. The person with the sore is unclean, and he must be put outside the camp. If the spot doesn't seem to go deep into the skin, and if the hair has not turned white, the condition may not be contagious. It is still too early to tell. The priest should put the affected person in a place by themselves for seven days. Then he will examine the spot again.

If, after seven days, the spot has not spread or become worse, the priest will simply have the person wash their skin and clothes. They are clean. If the rash does spread later on, that person must go back to the priest.

If a skin disease covers a person from head to foot, and if all their skin has turned white, the priest will call that person clean unless he sees raw flesh. When the raw flesh turns white, the priest will call them clean.

If a sore heals leaving behind a strange spot, the priest must examine the spot. He will see if a contagious skin disease has developed in place of the sore. When someone has a burn that doesn't seem to be healing correctly, the priest must examine it too.

When a person has a sore on their head or chin, the priest must examine it. If it seems to go below the top of the skin, and if the hair in the sore is affected, the priest will call the person unclean. Otherwise, as with other skin conditions, the priest will put that person by themselves for seven days and then examine the skin again.

Shiny white spots are signs of a contagious disease. Dull white spots are a harmless rash. If the priest sees that a person's spots are dull white, he will call that person clean.

A man who loses his hair is clean unless he has a reddish-white sore on the bald part of his head. If it is a swollen sore, he has a contagious skin disease. He is unclean.

For as long as a person is unclean, they must wear torn clothes and cover their face. They must live outside the camp, and they must warn anyone coming near them that they are unclean."

Discussion:

Why was a person separated when it was suspected that they might have a skin disease?

Is it right for a contagious person to be around the rest of the congregation? Does this apply only to physical health?

Part III: Leviticus 13:47-59

NT: Matthew 5:29-30

"If any piece of fabric or leather has a spot of greenish or reddish mold, it should be shown to the priest. The priest will put the fabric in a safe place for seven days; then he will look again. If the mold has spread, the material must be burned. If the mold has not spread, the material must be washed and then put back in a safe place for seven more days. If, after the seven days, the mold looks exactly like it did before, the material must be burned. If the spot is a lighter color, the priest will cut the spot out of the fabric and wash the rest of the fabric again. If the mold does not come back, the fabric is clean once it's been washed one more time."

Discussion:

Why is it so important to cut out the mold? How does this relate to our lives?

Part IV: Leviticus 14:1-57

NT: II Corinthians 6:14-7:1; Matthew 8:1-4

YHVH said to Moses, "If the priest hears that a person has been healed from a contagious skin disease, he must go outside the camp to check. If the person really has been healed, the priest will ask for two clean birds, cedar wood, bright red yarn, and hyssop. The priest will have one of the birds killed over a clay pot of clean water. Then he will wrap the live bird with the cedar wood, hyssop, and yarn, and he will dip it into the water and blood of the other bird. He will sprinkle the healed person seven times with the soaked bird, and then he will set the bird free. The one who has been healed is now clean. Once the cleaned person washes and shaves off all their hair, they may come back into the camp. They must then live outside their tent for seven more days. After seven days, they must shave again. Then they are clean. On the eighth day, the cleaned person must bring two perfect one-year-old rams and a perfect female lamb. With the lambs, the healed person must bring eleven-and-a-half pounds of fine flour mixed with oil and one-third of a quart of oil. The priest will present the offerings to YHVH. The priest will then take one of the rams and offer it as a guilt offering. He will wave the ram and the oil to YHVH, and then he will kill the ram where the purification and burned offerings are killed.

The priest will take some of the blood of the offering and put it on the right ear, right thumb, and right big toe of the healed person. Then the priest will take some of the oil that is still in his hand from the wave offering, and he will put it on the right ear, right thumb, and right big toe of the healed person. He will put the rest of the oil that is in his palm on the head of the healed person. Then the priest will offer the purification offering and the guilt offering with the grain offering, and the healed person will be clean. If the healed person cannot afford the animals he needs for the offerings, he may bring a lamb as the guilt offering and two doves or pigeons as the purification and burned offerings."

YHVH spoke to Moses and Aaron. He said, "When you are living in the land of Canaan and I put a plague of mold inside one of your houses, the owner must go and tell the priest. Everything inside the house should be removed before the priest goes in to inspect the mold. The priest will look for a greenish or reddish mold. If the mold seems to go deeper than the surface of the wall, the priest will lock up the house for seven days. Seven days later, if he looks and sees that the mold has spread, the priest will have all the moldy stones ripped out of the wall and taken outside the camp. The rest of the wall will be scraped clean, and the house will be rebuilt with clean stones and clay. If the mold spreads again, the house must be torn down.

Anyone who enters the house while it is closed will be unclean until evening. Anyone who sleeps or eats in the house must wash his clothes.

If the mold has not spread after seven days, the priest will say that the house is clean.

Once the house is clean, the priest will take two live birds, cedar wood, bright red yarn, and hyssop. He will sprinkle the house seven times—just like he did with the healed person. Then the house will be clean."

Discussion:

How important is it for our homes/our households to be clean?

Why would God send a plague of mold to someone's house?

Are dirt and mold the only ways a house can be dirty?

Part V: Leviticus 15:1-33

NT: Luke 8:43-48

[Mature content ahead.]

"If a man has any unusual fluid flowing from his body, he is unclean. Everyone who touches him will be unclean until evening. If he touches someone without washing his hands, they will be unclean until evening. Whatever he sits on or lies on will be unclean, and anyone who touches those things must take a bath. They will be unclean until evening. If the man spits on anyone who is clean, they must wash their clothes. They are unclean until evening. If the man touches a clay pot, the pot must be destroyed. Wooden things must be washed.

Once the fluid has stopped, the man must wait seven more days before he can be cleaned. On the eighth day, he must take two doves or pigeons to the priest. The priest will sacrifice them as a purification offering and a burned offering; then the man will be clean.

When a man sleeps with his wife and releases semen, he and his wife must take a bath. They will both be unclean until evening. Anything the semen touches must be washed. It is also unclean until evening.

When a woman has her monthly bleeding, she is unclean for seven days. Anything the blood touches will be unclean. Anyone who touches her will be unclean until evening. Anyone who touches her bed or chair must take a bath. They will be unclean until evening.

If a man sleeps with his wife and her monthly blood touches him, he will be unclean for seven days.

If a woman bleeds for a longer time than is normal, she will remain unclean as long as she is bleeding. Once the bleeding stops, she must wait seven days to be cleaned. On the eighth day, she will bring two doves or pigeons to the priest. He will sacrifice one as a purification offering and the other as a burned offering. Then she will be clean.

It is important to keep the Israelites away from anything unclean so that they do not die when they come into My Tabernacle."

Discussion:

Why is it so important not to touch an unclean thing or a person when they are unclean? What can we learn from this?

Acharei Mot (After the death) –
Leviticus 16:1 - 18:30; Ezekiel 22:1 - 19;
I Samuel 20:18-42

Kedoshim (Holy people) –
Leviticus 19:1 - 20:27; Ezekiel 20:2-20;
Amos 9:7-15

(In leap years these portions are read separately.)

Portion:

Part I: Leviticus 16:1-34

NT: Hebrews 2:14-18, 10, 13:7-16

After two of Aaron's sons died, YHVH gave Moses a message for Aaron. He said, "I appear in the cloud behind the curtain where the Ark of the Covenant is. To save Aaron's life, tell him not to come into the Most Holy Place whenever he wants to. Give him these rules to follow:

First, he must bring a bull as a purification offering and a ram as a burned offering for himself. The people of Israel must bring two male goats as a purification offering and one ram as a burned offering. Before sacrificing the animals, Aaron must take a bath and put on his linen tunic, linen underclothes, and linen turban.

After killing the bull as a purification offering for himself and his family, Aaron must carry a censer of burning coals from the altar with two handfuls of holy incense. He must carry it behind the curtain to the Most Holy Place. The smoke from the incense will hide the cover of the Ark so that Aaron will not be killed. Then Aaron will take some of the bull's blood with his finger; he will sprinkle it on the front of the atonement cover and seven more times in front of the cover.

Aaron must bring the people's goats to the front of the Tabernacle so that YHVH can choose between them. Aaron will kill the goat that YHVH chooses as a purification offering for the people. He will take some of its blood into the Most Holy Place just like he did with the bull's blood. He must also clean the rest of the Tabernacle and the altar this way. The Tabernacle and the Most Holy Place must be cleaned because of the people's sin. No one is allowed inside the Tabernacle while Aaron is making atonement.

After this, Aaron will lay his hands on the live goat's head and confess all the sin of the Israelites. He will send the goat into the wilderness carrying their sins away. Then Aaron will go back to the Tabernacle. He will take off his linen clothes, take a bath, and put back on his regular clothes. On the altar, he will burn the burned offerings and the fat from the purification offerings. The rest of the bull and goat that were sacrificed for purification must be burned outside the camp.

The man who took the goat into the wilderness may come back to the camp after he has washed his clothes and taken a bath. The man who burned the goat and bull outside the camp may also come back after he has washed his clothes and taken a bath.

This is what the high priest of Israel will do once a year on the tenth day of the seventh month. This day should be a holy Sabbath and a day of fasting for all the people of Israel."

Discussion:

What animals were brought as burned offerings?

What kept Aaron from dying when entering the Most Holy Place?

Why was Aaron supposed to call for two goats?

When was Aaron supposed to enter the Most Holy Place?

Why did the rest of the purification offerings need to be burned outside the camp (instead of being eaten by the priests)? Hint: Where had their blood been taken?

Part II: Leviticus 17:1-16

NT: John 6:43-59

YHVH spoke to Moses. He said, "Tell the people not to offer sacrifices in their fields. They may only make sacrifices by bringing the animal to the entrance of the Tabernacle. The priest must sprinkle the blood against the altar and burn the fat to YHVH. The Israelites are still tempted to sacrifice to the goat idols, and I will not allow this to continue. I will cut those people off from Israel.

Israelites must not eat meat with the blood still in it. The blood must be drained from the animals they eat because blood is sprinkled on the altar for their sake. If a clean animal is hunted and killed for food, its blood must be buried underground. Anyone who eats blood will be cut off from the people of Israel.

If anyone eats an animal that was killed by another animal, he should wash and change his clothes. He is unclean until evening."

Discussion:

Why were the people not allowed to sacrifice except in front of the Tabernacle?

Is a hunted animal a sacrifice?

Part III: Leviticus 18:1-30

NT: I Corinthians 5:1-5

[Mature content ahead.]

YHVH said to Moses, "I am YHVH. Tell the Israelites to follow My laws and to not act like the pagan nations. Say this to the people: 'Do not marry close family members or stepfamily members. Do not marry a mother and daughter. Do not marry your brother's wife while your brother is alive. Do not marry your wife's sister while your wife is alive. Men should marry women and women should marry men. Do not sacrifice your children to Molek. No one should be with an animal like they would be with their husband or wife.'

These are the things that the pagan nations do. Even the land they live in is ruined because of their sin, and I am driving them out of their land. You must keep My laws. Do not allow these terrible sins to infect the congregation of Israel. Anyone who acts this way will be cut off from Israel."

Discussion:

Why was God driving the pagan nations out of Canaan?

Part IV: Leviticus 19:1-37

NT: Romans 7, 13:8-10

YHVH spoke to Moses and gave him a message for the people. He said, "Be holy because I, YHVH, am holy.

Respect your father and mother.

Keep My Sabbaths.

Do not worship idols.

Eat a fellowship offering before the third day (on the day of the sacrifice or the next day).

Do not harvest the edges of your fields; leave food for the poor.

Do not steal.

Do not lie to or try to trick each other.

Do not swear in My name and then break your word.

Do not cheat each other.

Pay your employees right away.

Do not be mean to the disabled.

Treat everyone fairly whether they are rich or poor.

Do not say bad things behind each other's backs.

Do not put anyone's life in danger.

Do not hate a fellow Israelite. If they are sinning, you have to say something to them. Otherwise, you will also be guilty of their sin.

Do not hold a grudge or try to get revenge. Love your neighbor as yourself. I am YHVH.

Keep all My laws.

Do not breed two kinds of animals together.

Do not plant your fields with two kinds of seed.

Do not weave two types of fabric into the same piece of clothing.

If a man sleeps with a female slave who is supposed to marry someone else but has not been freed to marry, he must bring a guilt offering because he has done wrong.

When you plant a new tree in the land God is giving you, do not pick the fruit for the first three years. In the fourth year, the fruit will belong to YHVH as an offering. After that year, the fruit may be eaten.

Do not eat meat with blood in it.

Do not practice witchcraft or look for pagan signs.

Do not tear the corners of your beards or cut your bodies for the dead. Do not tattoo yourselves.

Do not make your daughters serve other gods.

Keep My Sabbath and My Tabernacle holy.

Do not ask for advice from witches or fortune tellers.

Honor the elderly. Stand up when an elderly person comes into the room.

Treat foreigners with kindness. Remember how you were treated in Egypt.

Be honest in all your trading and selling.

Keep all My laws. I am YHVH."

Discussion:

How many laws can you remember? Do you have trouble keeping any of these?

Part V: Leviticus 20:1-27

NT: I Corinthians 5

[Mature content ahead.]

YHVH gave Moses more laws for the Israelites:

"If you do not keep My laws, there will be consequences:

Anyone who sacrifices his children to Molek must be put to death.

No Israelite should ask for the advice of witches or fortune tellers. I will cut that person off from Israel.

Be set apart from the world, because I am YHVH your God. I make you holy.

Anyone who curses his father or mother should be put to death.

If a man and a woman are caught in adultery, they must be put to death.

Anyone who has a sexual relationship with a close family member must be put to death or removed from Israel.

If a man sleeps with a man like men do with women, both men must be put to death.

Anyone who has a sexual relationship with an animal must be put to death. You must also kill the animal.

If a man marries a close family member, they should be removed from Israel.

If a man sleeps with a woman even though he knows she is having her monthly bleeding, they must be cut off from Israel.

If a man marries his brother's wife while his brother is still alive, they will not have any children.

These are the things you must remember so you will be allowed to live in the land. I have set you apart from other people.

Remember the difference between clean and unclean animals, and do not make yourselves unholy.

If a man or a woman attempts to contact the dead, they must be put to death."

Discussion:

The nations around Israel were committing these sins. Why did God need to remind His own people not to commit them?

Emor (Speak) –
Leviticus 21:1 - 24:23; Ezekiel 44:15-31

Portion:

Part I: Leviticus 21:1-24

NT: II Corinthians 11:1-2; I Corinthians 6:12-20

YHVH said to Moses, "Speak to the priests, and let them know what I expect. When someone dies, a priest must not touch the dead body unless the person was an immediate family member of the priest. For close family members, he may make himself unclean. However, he must not grieve for the dead in pagan ways like shaving his head, tearing his beard, or cutting his body. The priests must always keep the name of YHVH holy.

Priests may only marry women who are pure. Even a legally divorced woman is not an appropriate wife for a priest.

The priests' children must also live holy lives.

The high priest is the one who has been anointed with oil and who wears the anointed clothes. Even if his parents die, the high priest must not enter the home where a dead body is. He must not tear his clothes or uncover his head even though he is sad.

The woman a high priest marries must be from his family. She must be completely pure. He may not marry a widow or anyone who has ever been with another man.

If a descendant of Aaron is not whole and healthy, he may not serve in the Tabernacle. He is allowed to eat the holy food reserved for the priests, but he may not offer sacrifices."

Discussion:

Yeshua is the Heavenly High Priest, and He is coming for a pure Bride from His own family. What can we learn from the passage that we can apply to our lives?

Part II: Leviticus 22:1-16

NT: Ephesians 2:18-20

YHVH said to Moses, "Tell Aaron and his sons to treat the offerings with respect. No one outside a priest's family is allowed to eat the holy offerings. If a priest buys a person with money, or if slaves are born in a priest's house, those people are part of his family. They may eat the holy offerings. If a priest's daughter marries someone who is not a priest, she may no longer eat the holy offerings. No one may eat the holy offerings while they are unclean. If a descendant of Aaron is unclean, he may not eat the holy offerings until he has been cleaned. If a person eats some of a holy offering by mistake, they must pay back what they ate plus one-fifth. The priests must not let this happen on purpose."

Discussion:

Who is allowed to eat from the offerings?

Part III: Leviticus 22:17-33

NT: II Corinthians 9

YHVH said to Moses, "Tell all the Israelites that if they want to bring YHVH a vow offering or a freewill offering, they must bring an ox, ram, or male goat that is healthy. They must not bring animals that are injured or sick. They may bring an ox, ram, or goat that is a runt or deformed, but they may only bring those animals as freewill offerings. They may not bring imperfect animals as vow offerings.

Do not sacrifice an animal unless it is at least eight days old. After the eighth day, it may be sacrificed—but not on the same day as its mother.

If you bring a thank offering to YHVH, eat all of it on the same day.

Keep My commands and follow them. I am YHVH who rescued you from Egypt."

Discussion:

What does YHVH expect from us? What kind of sacrifices did/does He require?

Part IV: Leviticus 23:1-24:9

NT: Matthew 26

"Work for six days and keep the Sabbath day holy. Do not do any work on it—no matter where you live. The Sabbath belongs to YHVH.

Passover begins on the afternoon of the fourteenth day of the first month. The Feast of Unleavened Bread begins on the fifteenth day, and it lasts for seven days. Do not eat anything with yeast during this time. On the first and seventh day of the Feast of Unleavened Bread, you should gather together. Do not work on the first or seventh day.

After you've entered the Promised Land and reaped your first harvest, you must bring a bundle of your first grain to YHVH. The priest will wave the grain to YHVH on the day after the Sabbath. On this same day, you must also bring a perfect one-year-old lamb as a burned offering with a grain offering of fine flour and oil and a drink offering of wine. You must not eat any of the new grain until this offering has been given to YHVH.

Starting on the day after the Sabbath when your first grain is waved to YHVH, begin counting seven weeks plus one day. Give new grain to YHVH on the fiftieth day. Bring two loaves of fine flour baked with yeast. With the bread, you must also bring seven perfect one-year-old lambs, one young bull, and two rams. Give these animals to YHVH as a burned offering. For a purification offering, sacrifice a male goat. For a fellowship offering, sacrifice two one-year-old lambs. The priest will wave the two lambs and the bread to YHVH.

Don't forget! When you harvest your fields, do not try to get every bit. Do not harvest the corners at all. That way, there will be enough food for the poor and the strangers in Israel.

Celebrate the first day of the seventh month by gathering together and blowing the trumpets. Present food offerings to YHVH, but do not do any regular work.

Gather together on the tenth day of the seventh month. This is the Day of Atonement when atonement is made for the people of Israel. Spend the day fasting and resting; do not eat or work. Offer a food offering to YHVH.

The Feast of Tabernacles starts on the fifteenth day of the seventh month. This feast lasts for seven days. Do not work on the first day. Offer food offerings to YHVH every day during the festival. After you have lived in the land and harvested crops, you will celebrate this feast. During the feast, live in temporary shelters to remind your children of your time in the wilderness. Take the branches of palms, willows, and leafy trees, and joyfully praise YHVH for the seven days of the feast. Gather together on the eighth day. It is also a Sabbath to YHVH."

YHVH said to Moses, "Command the Israelites to bring pure olive oil to keep the lamps in the lampstand burning. The lampstand is outside the curtain that guards the Ark of the Covenant. Aaron must take care of the lamps and always keep them burning.

Sabbath after Sabbath, bake twelve loaves made of fine flour, and place them on the gold table in the Tabernacle. The priests must eat this bread inside the Tabernacle. It is very holy."

Discussion:

On what day is the Feast of Passover?

When does Unleavened Bread begin?

Can you remember the order of the feast days? What feast is coming up next?

Part V: Leviticus 24:10-23

NT: Acts 6:8-15

One day, a man with an Israelite mother and an Egyptian father got into a fight with an Israelite. The man with the Egyptian father spoke a curse against the name of YHVH. The people brought the guilty man to Moses to decide what to do with him.

YHVH told Moses, "Tell the people to take the man outside the camp. Anyone who heard him speak the curse must put their hand on his head. All of Israel must stone him to death.

Anyone who curses or blasphemes the name of YHVH must be put to death.

Anyone who kills a human being must be put to death.

Anyone who kills someone's animal should pay for the animal. All crimes should be paid for according to the seriousness of the crime.

These laws apply to people born in Israel and to the outsiders who live in Israel's camp."

Discussion:

How is a crime paid for according to its seriousness? What does that mean?

Behar (On the Mount) –
Leviticus 25:1 - 26:2; Jeremiah 32:6-27

Bechukotai (By My regulations) –
Leviticus 26:3 - 27:34; Jeremiah 16:19 - 17:14

(In leap years these portions are read separately.)

Portion:

Part I: Leviticus 25:1-34

NT: Luke 4:14-21

YHVH gave Moses a message for the Israelites. He said, "When you enter the Promised Land, the land must also keep a Sabbath. Plant and harvest for six years, but let the land rest on the seventh year. Do not plant or harvest on the Sabbath year. You, your servants, foreigners, your livestock, and wild animals are allowed to eat the things that grow on their own, but do not plant or work in your fields.

Every seventh Sabbath year, after forty-nine years, blow the trumpet on the Day of Atonement (which is the tenth day of the seventh month). Make the fiftieth year a special year, and celebrate freedom throughout the land of Israel. The fiftieth year is the year of Jubilee. Do not plant or work in your fields. In the year of Jubilee, everyone will return to the land that was given to their tribe as an inheritance. Because you know that this will happen, do not take advantage of each other. When you sell land to your people, set the price based on how many years it is until the next Jubilee. It is the years of crops that you are selling—not the land itself. If Jubilee is near, the land is not worth as much.

Obey Me, and you will live safely in the land. The land will produce plenty of food so that you will never be hungry. Do not worry about what you will eat in the Sabbath years. I will cause what you plant in the sixth year to feed you for three years. You will eat from the harvest of the sixth year until it is time to harvest from the ninth year. You will always have enough.

The land must be redeemed in the year of Jubilee because the land is Mine. It is never to be sold permanently because it is My land.

If an Israelite becomes poor and sells his land to another Israelite for money, the buyer must allow the seller's close relative to come and buy back the land. If there isn't a relative to buy it back but the seller becomes able to buy it back for himself, the seller and the buyer should do the math to figure out how much the land is still worth until Jubilee. The seller will give the buyer that amount for the land. If the seller cannot buy back his land, he'll get it back when Jubilee comes.

If someone sells a house that is located inside a walled city, that house will not be returned in the year of Jubilee. However, the seller does have one year to buy back the house. If he has not redeemed it within that time, it will become the permanent property of the buyer and his descendants. Houses in villages without walls may be bought back at any time, and they will be returned in the year of Jubilee.

The Levites always have the right to redeem their homes that are located in Levite land, and their homes will always be returned in the year of Jubilee. The land in Levite cities must never be sold; it is the Levites' permanent possession."

Discussion:

The land should rest every _____ year?

What will the people eat on the seventh year?

When is the year of Jubilee?

When is a sold home not to be redeemed?

What land should never be sold?

Part II: Leviticus 25:35-54

NT: Luke 1:67-69

"If any of your Israelite neighbors become too poor to take care of themselves, the rest of the Israelites should care for them just like they should care for a foreigner. Do not charge Israelites interest. Do not make a profit off of helping them. I brought you out of Egypt. I am YHVH your God.

If an Israelite becomes so poor that he is forced to sell himself to another Israelite, he should not be forced to work as a slave. He should be treated fairly as a hired worker. In the Jubilee year, he will go free and back to the land that his ancestors inherited. You may have slaves from other nations, but you should not make any Israelite your slave.

If an Israelite becomes poor and sells himself to a foreigner living among the Israelites, a relative may redeem him. He may also redeem himself. If he is not redeemed, he will go free in the Year of Jubilee. Make sure he is not mistreated while he works for the foreigner. The Israelites are My servants; they should not be slaves to anyone. I brought them out of Egypt."

Discussion:

Is an Israelite allowed to make a slave of another Israelite?

Why would an Israelite sell himself to another Israelite?

Part III: Leviticus 26:1-13

NT: John 14:23-31

"Do not make any idols.

Keep My Sabbaths and honor My Tabernacle.

If you obey Me in everything I tell you to do, I will send rain at the right time and your crops will grow. You will always have plenty to eat.

I will give you peace. I will chase away the wild animals, and no one will hurt you. You will chase your enemies; they will not chase you. Large armies will run from just a small group of you.

You will have many children, and I will keep My covenant with you. I will live with you, and I will bless all your work. You will be My people. I am YHVH your God. I rescued you from your slavery in Egypt."

Discussion:

The covenant of YHVH will be with the people if _____. What did He tell His people to do?

Part IV: Leviticus 26:14-46

NT: Luke 13:1-9

"If you do not obey Me, if you say 'no' to My laws, I will bring terrible things to you. I will allow disease and fever to make you weak. You will plant seed, but your enemies will harvest the crops. I will not fight for you, and your enemies will defeat you.

If you still will not turn back to Me, I will punish you seven times worse than before. The sky will not rain; the ground will not grow a crop no matter how hard you work.

If you still disobey Me, I will punish you seven times worse than before. I will send wild animals to attack you. They will steal your children from you, and they will destroy your cattle; they will kill and destroy until only a few of you are left alive.

If you are still against Me, I will punish you seven times worse than before. I will send war and plagues, and I will give you to your enemies. You will always be hungry.

If this does not make you repent, I will punish you seven times worse than before. I will destroy everything living in the land, and your enemies will be shocked to see what has happened. The few of you who are left, I will scatter throughout the nations of the world where you will always be afraid. When you are gone from the land, then it will have the Sabbaths that you did not give it.

After all of this, if your children repent and turn back to Me, if they confess their sin and the sins of their fathers, I will remember My covenant with Abraham, Isaac, and Jacob. They will pay for their sins, but I will not reject them."

Discussion:

What did God say would happen to the Israelites if they did not keep His covenant?

How hard would YHVH try to get them to repent?

Could they repent and come back to Him?

Part V: Leviticus 27:1-34

NT: Romans 1:1-3

"If someone wants to dedicate a person to YHVH, they must pay the commanded price. If they cannot afford to pay the set price, the priest will set a price that they can afford.

If a person wants to dedicate a clean animal to YHVH, the animal becomes holy and will be sacrificed to YHVH. It cannot be traded for a better or a worse animal. If it *is* traded for another animal, both animals will be set apart for YHVH. If a person dedicates an unclean animal that cannot be sacrificed, the priest will decide what the animal is worth. If the person wants to keep their dedicated animal, they can buy it back for the full price plus one-fifth.

If someone wants to dedicate their house to YHVH, the priest will decide the value. If family land is dedicated, the value will be based on how much seed it takes to plant the land. The priest will also set the price based on the number of years until Jubilee. If the person offering the land wants to buy it back, he must pay full price plus one-fifth. If the land is not redeemed by the year of Jubilee, it permanently belongs to the priests.

If someone wants to dedicate a piece of land that is not theirs to keep after the year of Jubilee (it is not their family's land), the value will be lower and based on the number of years until Jubilee.

No one is allowed to dedicate something that already belongs to YHVH. The first-born sons and first-born male livestock already belong to YHVH. A tenth of everything belongs to YHVH. No one may switch something good for something bad when they are offering a tithe to YHVH."

Discussion:

What does it mean to dedicate something or someone to YHVH?

Bamidbar (In the desert) – Numbers 1:1 - 4:20; Hosea 2:1-22

Portion:

Part I: Numbers 1:1-54

NT: James 1:1

On the first day of the second month in the second year after the Israelites left Egypt, YHVH spoke to Moses. He asked him to count the Israelite men who were twenty years old or older and were able to fight in the army. He told him to write down their names. YHVH assigned respected leaders from each tribe to help Moses with this very big job. These are the men who were assigned to help:

From the tribe of Reuben, Elizur.

From the tribe of Simeon, Shelumiel.

From the tribe of Judah, Nahshon.

From the tribe of Issachar, Nethanel.

From the tribe of Zebulun, Eliab.

From Joseph's son Ephraim, Elishama.

From Joseph's son Manasseh, Gamaliel.

From the tribe of Benjamin, Abidan.

From the tribe of Dan, Ahiezer.

From the tribe of Asher, Pagiel.

From the tribe of Gad, Eliasaph.

From the tribe of Naphtali, Ahira.

With the help of the leaders, Moses and Aaron called the people together.

From the tribe of Reuben, they counted 46,500 fighting men.

From the tribe of Simeon, they counted 59,300 fighting men.

From the tribe of Gad, they counted 45,650 fighting men.

From the tribe of Judah, they counted 74,600 fighting men.

From the tribe of Issachar, they counted 54,400 fighting men.

From the tribe of Zebulun, they counted 57,400 fighting men.

From the half-tribe of Ephraim, they counted 40,500 fighting men.

From the half-tribe of Manasseh, they counted 32,200 fighting men.

From the tribe of Benjamin, they counted 35,400 fighting men.

From the tribe of Dan, they counted 62,700 fighting men.

From the tribe of Asher, they counted 41,500 fighting men.

From the tribe of Naphtali, they counted 53,400 fighting men.

At that time, there were 603,550 fighting men in Israel.

YHVH told Moses not to count the Levites with the rest of Israel. The Levites had a special job. When it was time for the Israelites to move from one place to another, it was the Levites' job to take down and set up the Tabernacle and all its pieces. The rest of the Israelites were assigned camping spots by tribe, but the Levites were told to camp in a circle around the Tabernacle and to protect the Israelites from the presence of YHVH.

Discussion:

Which of the Israelites were to be counted by name?

How many tribes were counted?

Part II: Numbers 2:1-34

NT: Revelation 21:9-14

Moses and Aaron told the Israelites how YHVH wanted them to set up their campsites: No one was allowed to camp very close to the Tabernacle. Under the flag of the tribe of Judah, the tribes of Issachar, Zebulun, and Judah were told to camp on the east side of the Tabernacle. When it was time for Israel to move, the tribes under Judah's flag would lead the way. There were 186,400 fighting men in that group.

On the south side of the Tabernacle, the tribes of Simeon, Gad, and Reuben were told to camp under Reuben's flag. When it was time for Israel to move, the south side tribes would be second in line. There were 151,450 fighting men in that group.

The Levites were told to camp around the Tabernacle between the Tabernacle and the rest of the Israelites. When it was time to move, the Levites would break down the Tabernacle and travel in the middle of the Israelites.

On the west side of the Tabernacle, the tribes of Manasseh, Benjamin, and Ephraim were told to camp under Ephraim's flag. They were next in line when it was time to move. There were 108,100 fighting men in that group.

On the north side of the Tabernacle, the tribes of Asher, Naphtali, and Dan were told to camp under Dan's flag. They were last in line when it was time to move. There were 157,600 fighting men in that group.

Discussion:

Did God care where each tribe camped or in which order they moved?

Why do you think YHVH arranged the tribes the way He did? Do you see any kind of pattern?

Part III: Numbers 3:1-38

NT: John 2:18-22

Aaron had four sons, but Nadab and Abihu died when they brought an offering to YHVH that He did not allow. Now Eleazar and Ithamar, Aaron's two living sons, served as priests with their father.

YHVH told Moses to give the tribe of Levi to Aaron. They would be helpers for their brothers, the priests. The Levites were told to serve the priests and the Tabernacle by taking care of the holy things. If anyone else came into the sanctuary of YHVH, they would die.

YHVH told Moses, "I planned to choose the first-born son from every Israelite family, but now I choose the tribe of Levi instead. All the first-born sons belong to Me because I set them apart when I killed the first-born in Egypt."

Then YHVH told Moses to count every Levite male who was one month old or older.

The sons of Levi were named Gershon, Kohath, and Merari.

In the tribe of Gershon, also called the Gershonites, were the families of Libni and Shimei. The Gershonites were told to camp to the west behind the Tabernacle. They were responsible for the Tabernacle coverings, the entrance curtain, the courtyard curtains, the curtain surrounding the Tabernacle and altar, as well as the ropes and anything related to these things. The number of Gershonite males was 7,500. Their leader's name was Eliasaph; he was the son of Lael.

In the tribe of Kohath, also called the Kohathites, were the families of Amram, Izhar, Hebron, and Uzziel. The Kohathites were told to camp on the south side of the Tabernacle. They were responsible for the ark, the lampstand, the altars, the articles used for sacrifices and ministering, and the curtain surrounding the ark. The number of Kohathite males was 8,600. Their leader's name was Elizaphan; he was the son of Uzziel.

In the tribe of Merari, also called the Merarites, were the families of Mahli and Mushi. The Merarites were told to camp on the north side of the Tabernacle. They were responsible for the frame of the Tabernacle as well as the posts, tent pegs, and ropes of the outer courtyard curtain. The number of Merarite males was 6,200. Their leader's name was Zuriel; he was the son of Abihail.

Moses and Aaron and his sons were told to camp on the east side of the Tabernacle. They were the only ones allowed to work in the sanctuary. If anyone else tried to do the jobs given to Moses and to Aaron and his sons, they would die.

Discussion:

Which Levite family would you want to belong to? Which family do you think received the most honor? Which family had the hardest job?

Part IV: Numbers 3:39-51

NT: Colossians 1

Because YHVH decided to take the Levites for Himself (instead of taking the first-born sons of Israel), He commanded Moses to see how many first-born sons there were in Israel. Moses counted, and there were 22,273 non-Levite first-born males who were over one-month old. There were 22,000 Levite males over one-month old.

YHVH said to Moses, "Take all the Levite sons and the Levite livestock instead of the first-born of Israel. Because there are 273 more first-borns than there are Levites, those 273 must be redeemed. Collect five shekels for each one, and give the money to Aaron and his sons."

Discussion:

Why do you think YHVH chose the Levites instead of the first-born males of Israel? What had the Levites done to receive this honor? What had the rest of Israel done to lose this honor?

Part V: Numbers 4:1-20

NT: I Peter 1:1-13

YHVH commanded Moses to count the Kohathite men who were between thirty and fifty years old. They would serve in the Tabernacle when it was time for the Israelites to move. The Kohathites were in charge of moving the most holy things.

Before the Kohathites could come into the Tabernacle, Aaron and his sons were commanded to take down the curtain that shielded the Ark of the Covenant and to lay it over the Ark. Over the curtain, they were commanded to lay a piece of durable leather. Finally, they were commanded to cover the entire thing with a blue cloth and to make sure the carrying poles were secure.

Aaron and his sons were also commanded to cover the holy table with a blue cloth and to place the plates, dishes, bowls, jars, and bread on top. They were commanded to cover the blue cloth with a bright red cloth and to put a durable leather cloth on top of that. Lastly, they were commanded to slide the carrying poles into place.

They were commanded to cover the lampstand and its lamps with a blue cloth, wrap it in durable leather, and place it in a carrying frame. Then they were commanded to spread a blue cloth over the golden altar, place durable leather on top, and slide the carrying poles into place. They were commanded to take all the things used for worship and wrap them in a blue cloth, cover that with durable leather, and place the bundle into a carrying frame.

They were commanded to remove the ashes from the bronze altar and place all of the articles used for sacrificing on the altar. Lastly, they were commanded to cover the altar with durable leather and slide the carrying poles into place.

When all the holy things were covered, the Kohathites were allowed to come into the Tabernacle to carry the holy things by their carrying frames and poles. They were not allowed to touch the holy things themselves. YHVH commanded Moses and Aaron to give very careful instructions to the Kohathites so they would not die by looking at or touching the holy things.

Aaron's son Eleazar was responsible for the lamp oil, the incense, the grain offering, and the anointing oil. He was also in charge of everything that happened when they moved the Tabernacle.

Discussion:

How important was it that the priests cover the holy things before the Kohathites came in to move them?

Who saw the beauty of the things in the Tabernacle?

Nasso (Take) – Numbers 4:21 - 7:89; Judges 13:2-25

Portion:

Part I: Numbers 4:21-49

NT: Luke 1:5-25

YHVH also commanded Moses to count the Gershonite and the Merarite men who were thirty to fifty years old. Aaron's son Ithamar was in charge of giving orders to the Gershonites and the Merarites.

The number of Kohathite men ages thirty to fifty was 2,750.

The number of Gershonite men ages thirty to fifty was 2,630.

The number of Merarite men ages thirty to fifty was 3,200.

The total number of Levite men who were able to serve in the work of the Tabernacle was 8,580. YHVH told Moses what each man should carry.

Discussion:

Why was it important to count the Levites even though they were not part of the army?

Part II: Numbers 5:1-10

NT: Luke 10:25-33, 19:1-10

YHVH said, "Remember that anyone with a contagious skin disease or discharge and anyone who has been around a dead body must be sent away from the camp because I also live in the camp of Israel." The Israelites obeyed.

YHVH taught the Israelites how to repent when they hurt another person. He said to Moses, "First, they must confess their sin and then pay for the pain and loss plus one-fifth of the amount of the loss. If the person they wronged is now dead and there is no close relative to receive the payment, they must give the payment to the priest because it belongs to YHVH. Along with the payment, the one who did wrong must bring a ram to the priest."

Discussion:

What did YHVH command His people to do when they repented for hurting someone?

Part III: Numbers 5:11-31

NT: I Corinthians 4:1-5

YHVH said, "If a man suspects that his wife has not been faithful to him but there are no witnesses to prove whether he is right or wrong, he may bring her to the priest for a trial. He must bring with them three-and-a-half pounds of barley flour. He should not put oil or incense on the flour because it is a grain offering for jealousy. He is asking God to reveal his wife's sin.

The priest will bring the woman before YHVH. He will put holy water in a clay jar and put dust from the Tabernacle floor into the water. He will take down the woman's hair and place the grain offering in her hands. While holding the water, he will say to her, 'If you have not been unfaithful to your husband, may this water not bring a curse. But if you have sinned, may your stomach swell and may you never have children.' Then the woman must say, 'So be it.'

The priest will write down this curse and wash it off into the water. Then he will take the grain from her hands and wave it to YHVH. He will burn a handful of the grain on the altar. After this, the woman will drink the water. If she is innocent, she will have children; if not, she will be cursed."

Discussion:

All through Scripture, Israel is told to be faithful to YHVH and to keep His covenant. She is His Bride. Was/is she a faithful Bride?

Part IV: Numbers 6:1-27

NT: Acts 18; Acts 21

YHVH said to Moses, "If an Israelite man or woman wants to set themselves apart to serve Me in a special way, they may take a Nazirite vow. During this vow, they must not drink anything fermented or eat any part of the grape. During the time of the vow, they must not have a haircut. During the time of the vow, they must not go near a dead body— even if a close relative has died. If someone dies near them so that they cannot help being around a body, they must shave their head on the seventh day and start the same vow over again. They must also bring two doves or pigeons as a purification offering and a burned offering and one one-year-old ram as a guilt offering.

When their vow is over, they must go to the entrance of the Tabernacle. They must bring a perfect one-year-old lamb as a burned offering, a one-year-old female lamb as a purification offering, and a perfect ram for a fellowship offering. They must also bring a grain offering, a drink offering, and a basket of thick and thin unleavened bread made with oil.

After the priest has presented the offerings to YHVH, the one who has taken the vow must shave off the hair that grew during their special time of dedication. They must burn it with the fellowship offering. Then the priest will wave the shoulder of the ram with a thick and a thin loaf of bread. They belong to the priest as do the breast and thigh. After this, the vow will be finished, and the man or woman may drink wine and eat grapes. If a vow is made to YHVH, it must be kept."

Then YHVH said to Moses, "Teach Aaron and his sons how to bless the Israelites. Tell them to say:

'YHVH bless you and keep you. YHVH make His face shine on you and be kind to you. YHVH turn His face to you and give you peace.'

They will put My name on the Israelites, and I will bless them."

Discussion:

Why would a person want to take a Nazarite vow?

How can we dedicate ourselves to YHVH today?

Part V: Numbers 7:1-89

NT: Mark 12:41-44

After the Tabernacle was set up and dedicated, every tribe brought an offering to YHVH. First the leaders got together and brought carts and oxen to YHVH. They brought a total of six carts pulled by twelve oxen. YHVH told Moses to give the carts and oxen to the Levites because they would need them in their work. The Gershonites received two carts and the Merarites received four carts. The Kohathites did not receive any carts because they were commanded to carry the holy things on their shoulders by carrying poles.

Each tribe's leader brought one silver plate that weighed about three and a quarter pounds and one silver bowl that weighed about one and three-quarter pounds. The bowls and plates were filled with fine flour mixed with oil as a grain offering. Each leader also brought a gold dish filled with incense. They brought one young bull, one ram, and a one-year-old ram as a burned offering. They brought one male goat as a purification offering. They brought two oxen, five rams, five male goats, and five one-year-old rams; all of these were sacrificed for a fellowship offering. They brought these things as an offering from their entire tribe.

The tribe of Judah brought their offering on the first day.

The tribe of Issachar brought their offering on the second day.

The tribe of Zebulun brought their offering on the third day.

The tribe of Reuben brought their offering on the fourth day.

The tribe of Simeon brought their offering on the fifth day.

The tribe of Gad brought their offering on the sixth day.

The tribe of Ephraim brought their offering on the seventh day.

The tribe of Manasseh brought their offering on the eighth day.

The tribe of Benjamin brought their offering on the ninth day.

The tribe of Dan brought their offering on the tenth day.

The tribe of Asher brought their offering on the eleventh day.

And the tribe of Naphtali brought their offering on the twelfth day.

When Moses entered the Tabernacle, he spoke with YHVH. YHVH spoke to Moses from between the cherubim on the cover of the Ark of the Covenant.

Discussion:

Why couldn't the Kohathites carry the holy things in carts?

How is a holy thing different from an everyday good thing?

Beha'alotcha (When you set up) – Numbers 8:1 - 12:16; Zechariah 2:14 - 4:7

Portion:

Part I: Numbers 8:1-26

NT: Titus 2:11-14

YHVH spoke to Moses. He said, "Tell Aaron that the lamps in the stand must face forward and light the area in front of the stand."

Then YHVH told Moses to separate the Levites from the rest of the Israelites. As YHVH commanded, Moses sprinkled the Levites with cleansing water. He told them to shave their whole bodies and to wash their clothes. YHVH also commanded the Levites to bring a young bull along with a grain offering and another bull as a purification offering.

Moses called the Levites to the front of the Tabernacle. Then the Israelites laid their hands on the Levites, and Aaron presented the Levites to YHVH. The Levites placed their hands on the bulls and offered their sacrifices to YHVH. As soon as they were cleaned and presented to YHVH, the Levites began doing the jobs that YHVH had assigned them to do. YHVH chose the Levites instead of every first-born son of an Israelite. YHVH commanded all Levite men who were at least twenty-five years old to begin serving the priests. The Levites were commanded to stop working when they turned fifty. They could help the younger Levites, but they could not continue doing their jobs after they turned fifty years old.

Discussion:

How were the Levites separated from the other Israelites?

How long was a Levite to serve in the Tabernacle work?

Part II: Numbers 9:1-23

NT: Matthew 17:4-6; I Corinthians 10:1-4

Soon it was the first month of the year again. It was the second year the Israelites had been free people, and it was almost time to celebrate the Passover. YHVH said to Moses, "Make sure the people celebrate the Passover exactly as I commanded." The people obeyed, and they celebrated Passover on the fourteenth day of the first month. However, some of the Israelites had been near a dead body and were not allowed to eat the Passover meal. They told Moses that it was unfair for them to miss the Passover offering, and Moses talked to YHVH about their problem. YHVH told Moses that if anyone was not able to keep the Passover because they were unclean or out of town, they could celebrate a second Passover one month later. Anyone who was able to keep the Passover but chose not to would be cut off from Israel. This and all Passover laws were for all the people—whether they had been born as Israelites or were traveling with the Israelites.

On the day the Tabernacle was set up, the pillar of cloud moved in. The pillar was fire at night and a cloud of smoke during the day. Whenever it was time for the Israelites to move, the cloud lifted and moved. The Israelites always followed the cloud whether it moved after a year or only a day. The Israelites camped where YHVH said to camp, and they moved when YHVH said to move.

Discussion:

What would keep someone from being able to eat the Passover meal?

If someone was not able to eat the Passover because of uncleanness or travel, would they have to wait for the next year's feast?

Part III: Numbers 10:1-36

NT: Matthew 24:29-31

YHVH commanded Moses to make two silver trumpets. The trumpets were used to communicate with the Israelites. The priests would blow the trumpets at feast times, when it was time to move, when it was time for the leaders to gather at the Tabernacle, when it was time for all the Israelites to gather at the Tabernacle, and when it was time for battle. There were different ways to blow the trumpets for each signal.

The first time the Israelites took down the Tabernacle and moved, it was the twentieth day of the second month in the Israelites' second year since leaving Egypt. When the cloud lifted, they moved. YHVH led the people from Sinai into to the Desert of Paran. The Israelites broke down their tents and the Tabernacle exactly as God told Moses. Each tribe left in the order they were commanded, and the Levites carried the Tabernacle just like they had been told. The Ark of the Covenant led the way, and Moses said, "Rise, YHVH, and scatter Your enemies! May Your enemies run from Your presence." When the Ark was set down, Moses said, "Come back, YHVH, to Your many, many people, Israel."

Discussion:

How did the Israelites know when it was time to move?

Part IV: Numbers 11:1-35

NT: Philippians 3:18-20; I Corinthians 14:1-3

The people began to complain, and YHVH was angry. Fire from YHVH burned the edges of the Israelites' camp. Moses prayed to YHVH, and the fire died down. They called the place *Taberah*, which means "burning."

Then the people complained about food. They said, "We had better things to eat in Egypt! We are so tired of manna!" Moses asked YHVH, "Why am I the one You chose to babysit these people? They are not my children. Should I be the only man responsible for all of them?"

YHVH told Moses to gather the seventy elders. He said, "I will take some of My spirit that I have put on you, and I will put it on them. They will share your job. Now tell the people to prepare themselves. They will have meat to eat until it makes them sick."

Moses asked, "Where will You find enough meat to feed all these people?"

YHVH answered and said, "Is there anything too difficult for Me?"

Moses called the seventy elders, but only sixty-eight of them came. YHVH poured His spirit on the elders, and they began to prophesy. After that day, they didn't prophesy again. The two elders who had not come with the others began to prophesy too. When Joshua heard the two men prophesying, he asked Moses to make them stop. Moses said, "Don't worry for my sake. I don't want to be the only prophet. I wish all of God's people were prophets."

Then a strong wind blew many quail toward the camp. The quail rested in a thick layer on the ground, and the people picked them up. When they had just started to eat, YHVH became angry. He struck the people with a plague. Everyone who had complained for meat died. They named the place *Kibroth Hattaavah*, which means "craving." After they left Kibroth Hattaavah, they traveled to Hazeroth.

Discussion:

How did YHVH answer the people's complaining?

Part V: Numbers 12:1-15

NT: James 4:10-12

Because Moses had married a foreign woman, Miriam and Aaron talked badly about him. "Don't we hear God too?" they said.

YHVH heard them talking, and He called them to the Tabernacle. He called Moses there, too. He said, "I talk to prophets through dreams and visions, but I talk clearly with Moses. He sees the form of YHVH. You should be afraid to speak against him." Then YHVH left them, and they saw that Miriam's skin was infected with leprosy. Moses cried out to YHVH, and he asked God to heal her. YHVH answered, "She has been dishonored. Put her outside the camp for seven days."

The Israelites did not move until Miriam was healed and back in the camp.

Discussion:

Why do you think Miriam's skin was infected instead of Aaron's?

Shelach (Send on your behalf) – Numbers 13:1 - 15:41; Joshua 2:1-24

Portion:

Part I: Numbers 13:1-25

NT: Matthew 14:22-36

YHVH told Moses to send twelve leaders, one man from each tribe, to go and explore the land He had promised to give them.

From Reuben, Moses chose Shammua, Zakkur's son.

From Simeon, Moses chose Shaphat, Hori's son.

From Judah, Moses chose Caleb, Jephunneh's son.

From Issachar, Moses chose Igal, Joseph's son.

From Ephraim, Moses chose Hoshea, Nun's son. (Moses changed Hoshea's name to Joshua.)

From Benjamin, Moses chose Palti, Raphu's son.

From Zebulun, Moses chose Gaddiel, Sodi's son.

From Manasseh, Moses chose Gaddi, Susi's son.

From Dan, Moses chose Ammiel, Gemalli's son.

From Asher, Moses chose Sethur, Michael's son.

From Naphtali, Moses chose Nahbi, Vophsi's son.

From Gad, Moses chose Geuel, Maki's son.

These are the men that Moses chose. Moses told the men to check out the land. He said, "Go through Negev and up to the mountains. See what kind of land Canaan is and what kind of people live there. How is the soil? Bring back some of the fruit that is growing there."

The men went and explored the land for forty days. They explored from the Desert of Zin all the way to Rehob toward Lebo Hamath. They went up through the Negev to Hebron where the children of Anak lived. When they reached the valley, they cut a large bunch of grapes that took two men to carry. They named the place *Valley of Eshkol*, because Eshkol means "cluster." They also collected pomegranates and figs to bring them back to the people.

Discussion:

How many men were sent to explore the land?

What did the men bring back with them?

Why do you think YHVH wanted the men to explore the land?

Do you think the men followed Moses's directions? Where did he ask them to go?

Part II: Numbers 13:26-14:12

NT: Philippians 4:4-9

When the men returned from exploring, they told the rest of the Israelites what they had seen. They told them how wonderful the land was, but they also told them terrifying things about the people who lived there. "We saw powerful people in walled cities. We could never defeat them," they said. But Caleb said, "We should go in and take the land! We can do it!"

"No, we can't!" the other men said. "We were like grasshoppers compared to the people there!"

When the Israelites heard this, they were very afraid. "We should have stayed in Egypt!" they said. "Now these people will kill us and take our wives and children! We should choose a leader to take us back to Egypt!"

Moses and Aaron fell on their faces in front of the Israelites. Joshua and Caleb tore their clothes, and they said to the people, "If YHVH is pleased with us, He will give us the good land. Do not be afraid of the people who live there. God is not with them; He is with us!"

The Israelites wanted to stone them. Then the glory of YHVH appeared to all the Israelites. YHVH said to Moses, "How long will these people treat Me this way? I will destroy them and build a better nation through you!"

Discussion:

Do you think things would have turned out differently if all the explorers had the faith of Joshua and Caleb? How?

Part III: Numbers 14:13-45

NT: Hebrews 3:7-19

Moses begged YHVH not to destroy the people. He said, "Do not do this, YHVH! The Egyptians will hear about it, and they will tell everyone that You are a God who breaks His word. They will say, 'He promised to lead them to a land of their own, but instead He killed them on the way there.' Forgive them, God, because You are loving and merciful."

YHVH said, "I have forgiven them for your sake, but no one who has complained against Me will ever enter the land. I will bring Joshua and Caleb into the land, but the entire congregation of Israel will wander in the wilderness until everyone who grumbled dies. Everyone who was counted in the census—everyone over twenty years old who complained against Me—will die. Their children will suffer in the wilderness for forty years because of their parents' sin; then *they* will enter the land."

YHVH sent a plague that killed the ten spies who brought bad news to the people. When the people heard about their deaths, they cried, "We have sinned! We know we were wrong, and now we want to enter the land!"

Moses warned them not to go to the land. "YHVH is not with you!" he said.

The Ark did not go with them, but the people went anyway. They were defeated. The Canaanites and the Amalekites pushed them all the way to Hormah.

Discussion:

Why were the explorers killed by the plague right away and disciplined more harshly than the rest of the Israelites?

The people decided to go to the land because that is what YHVH had told them to do before they sinned against Him. Do you think they realized that He would not go with them?

Part IV: Numbers 15:1-31

NT: Luke 23:33-34

YHVH said to Moses, "Tell the Israelites that when they are in the land and they bring Me a burned offering or vow offering from their herd or flock, they must also bring a grain offering and a drink offering with it. When they bring a lamb or goat, they must bring two quarts of fine flour mixed with one quart of olive oil as a grain offering and one quart of wine as a drink offering.

When they bring a ram, they must bring four quarts of fine flour mixed with one-and-a-quarter quarts of olive oil as a grain offering and one-and-a-quarter quarts of wine as a drink offering.

When they bring a young bull, they must bring six quarts of fine flour mixed with two quarts of olive oil as a grain offering and two quarts of wine as a drink offering.

When these offerings are burned, they smell good to YHVH. Do this for every bull, ram, lamb, and goat that you bring. This is the offerings law for people who were born as Israelites and for the strangers who live with you. There will be one Law for all people.

When you enter the land, present the first of your harvest to YHVH. Before you eat the food of the land, present some of it as an offering to YHVH.

The whole community of Israel might accidentally sin. Once they realize their mistake, the whole community must offer a young bull with its grain and drink offering as well as a male goat for a purification offering. The priest will offer the sacrifice for their forgiveness, and they will be forgiven because they didn't know what they were doing.

If one person sins accidentally, they must offer a one-year-old female goat.

This applies to everyone living in the community of Israel: those born as Israelites and those traveling with you. Anyone who hates YHVH's laws and sins in a rebellious way will be cut off from Israel."

Discussion:

Why were these things to be offered *after* entering the land?

Discuss unintentional sin.

Part V: Numbers 15:32-41

NT: Matthew 9:19-22

One day, an Israelite man gathered wood on the Sabbath day. YHVH ordered that the man be put to death, and the community of Israel took him outside the camp and stoned him.

Then YHVH said to Moses, "Tell the Israelites to wear tassels with a blue cord on the corners of their clothing. They will look at the tassels and remember My commandments. They will remember not to sin and to act like a holy people. Remember, I am YHVH your God who brought you out of Egypt."

Discussion:

Why was it so important to not let "small" Sabbath breaking continue?

What is the purpose of tassels?

Korach (Korah) –
Numbers 16:1 - 18:32; I Samuel 11:14 - 12:22

Portion:

Part I: Numbers 16:1-40

NT: Romans 13:1-7

Korah, who was a Levite from the family of Kohath, spoke badly about Moses. With him were three Rubenites named Dathan, Abiram, and On. These men talked 250 Israelite leaders into joining them in their anger against Moses and Aaron. When they came to Moses and Aaron, they said, "All of Israel is holy to God. What gives you the right to think you are better than the rest of us?"

When Moses heard their words, he fell on his face before YHVH. Then he said to the men, "In the morning, YHVH will show who is holy and who is not. He will choose who is allowed to come near Him. Every one of you should take a censer, put burning coals and incense in it, and take it to YHVH. Whoever YHVH chooses will be holy."

Then Moses rebuked Korah and the other Levites who were with him. Moses said, "YHVH has already called you to a special work and brought you closer to Him than the other Israelites! Isn't that good enough for you? You're not complaining against Aaron; your complaint is with YHVH."

Moses called for Dathan and Abiram, but they refused to come. They whined at Moses and said, "You took us from a land that flowed with milk and honey, and you brought us to the wilderness to die. Now you call to us like we are slaves? No. We won't come."

Moses was angry, and he said to YHVH, "I have never wronged them. Please do not accept any offering from them."

Moses told Korah and his followers to bring their censers to the Tabernacle when Aaron brought his censer. When Korah and his followers arrived at the tent, the glory of YHVH showed up. YHVH told Moses and Aaron, "Get away from the Israelites quickly so that I can kill them!"

Moses and Aaron begged God for the people. They said, "Please do not punish all of them because of Korah." YHVH said, "Move the rest of the people away from Korah, Dathan, and Abiram's tents. Moses obeyed. Then Moses announced to all the people, "If these men die of natural causes, YHVH has not judged them, and He has not sent me to lead you. But if something new happens, if the earth swallows these men, everything they own, and everyone who is on their side, then you will know that these men have disrespected YHVH."

When Moses finished talking, the earth opened up and swallowed the rebellious men along with their families and all their possessions. The Israelites screamed in fear. Then fire from YHVH came and destroyed those who were not allowed to bring Him incense (all 250—only Aaron lived because YHVH allowed him to come close).

YHVH spoke to Moses. Then Moses told Eleazar, son of Aaron, to gather the censers from the dead men and to dump the coals outside the camp. "The censers are holy. Hammer them into sheets, and cover the altar with them. They will be a sign to all the people that only descendants of Aaron are allowed to offer incense to YHVH."

Discussion:

What other story of unauthorized incense does this remind you of?

Who set up the authority in Israel? Who decided who could come near YHVH and who couldn't?

What do you think happened to On? Why wasn't he punished with the others?

Part II: Numbers 16:41-50

NT: Romans 8:26-34

The men who died had been respected in the camp. The next day, after the shock of their deaths wore off, the Israelites were angry at Moses and Aaron. They blamed them for the deaths of their friends. When they gathered to yell at Moses and Aaron, the cloud covered the Tabernacle and the glory of YHVH showed up. Once again, YHVH said to Moses and Aaron, "Get away from the people so that I can destroy them." Again, Moses and Aaron fell on their faces before YHVH.

Moses told Aaron, "Anger has come from YHVH, and a plague has started to spread through the camp. Quickly, take your censer with incense and coals from the altar, and make things right between the people and God!" Aaron ran to obey Moses. The plague had started, and people were dying quickly. Aaron stood between the dead and the living, and he stopped the plague from going any farther. 14,700 people died before Aaron reached the center of the plague.

Discussion:

What was Aaron's job as the high priest?

Part III: Numbers 17:1-11

NT: Philippians 2:1-18

YHVH commanded Moses to collect twelve staffs from the Israelites: one staff from the leader of each tribe. He commanded them to write the name of the leader on his staff. Aaron's name was written on the tribe of Levi's staff. YHVH commanded, and the men placed their staffs in the Tabernacle in front of the Ark of the Covenant. Moses said, "YHVH will show who He has chosen by causing the staff of that man to come to life with new growth. YHVH Himself will settle this argument over who is in charge and who isn't."

The men obeyed, and the next day they saw that Aaron's staff had budded, blossomed, and produced almonds. Each man took back his own staff, but YHVH commanded that Aaron's staff be placed in front of the Ark as a reminder against rebellion.

Discussion:

Why did Aaron's staff bud? Why did it bud so abundantly?

Part IV: Numbers 17:12-18:7

NT: I Thessalonians 3:12-13

The people were very afraid. They cried to Moses because so many had died. "If we even go near the Tabernacle, we will die!"

YHVH reminded Aaron, "You and your sons are responsible for the Tabernacle and the priesthood. Have the Levites help you, but do not let them touch anything in the Holy Place. You are responsible for protecting the rest of the Israelites. The priesthood belongs to you."

Discussion:

Why were Aaron and his sons in charge of the Tabernacle?

Part V: Numbers 18:8-32

NT: Hebrews 7

YHVH also reminded Aaron of the Levites' rights to the tithes and offerings: The priests and their sons were given the meat from the holy offerings—except for the parts that were burned to YHVH. The priests' sons and daughters were given the meat set aside from the gift and wave offerings. If they were clean, they could eat it. The wine and oil that the Israelites gave as first fruits offerings to YHVH belonged to the Levites. Every first-born male, both human and animal, also belonged to the Levites. Every first-born son and unclean animal would be redeemed for five shekels of silver. Every first-born cow, sheep, or goat would be offered to YHVH: its blood would be sprinkled on the altar. Whatever was set aside belonged to the Levites and to their sons and daughters.

YHVH said to Aaron for all the Levites, "You will have no inheritance in the land; I am your inheritance. All the tithes of Israel belong to you. It is your payment for serving Me. You are the only ones allowed to serve Me in the Tabernacle. When you receive a tithe from the Israelites, you must also tithe by offering ten percent to YHVH. Present the best part to YHVH, and you and your families may have the rest."

Discussion:

What did the Levites receive in exchange for their service to YHVH?

Chukat (Regulations) –
Numbers 19:1 - 22:1; Judges 11:1-33

Balak –
Numbers 22:2 - 25:9; Micah 5:6 - 6:8

(In leap years these portions are read separately.)

Portion:

Part I: Numbers 19:1-22

NT: Hebrews 10:22; Revelation 7:14

YHVH said to Moses and Aaron, "Tell the Israelites that they must find a perfect, young, red cow that has never been used for work, and they must give it to Eleazar the priest. The young cow will be taken outside the camp and killed in front of the priest. After it has been killed, Eleazar will take some of the cow's blood on his finger and sprinkle it seven times toward the Tabernacle. He will watch while the entire cow is burned. While it is still burning, the priest will take cedar wood, hyssop, and bright red wool—throwing them in to burn with the cow. Then the priest will wash his clothes and take a bath. He may come into the camp once he has bathed, but he will still be unclean. He cannot work in the Tabernacle until evening.

A man who is clean must gather up the ashes of the cow and put them in a clean place outside the camp. The man who gathers the ashes must also wash his clothes. He is unclean until evening.

Some of the ashes will be mixed with water, and this water will be used for making people clean after they have become unclean.

If someone touches a dead body, a human bone, or a grave, they are unclean for seven days. They must be sprinkled with purification water on the third day and on the seventh day. If they are not sprinkled on both days, they will no longer be part of Israel.

To purify an unclean person, put some of the ashes into a jar and pour fresh water over them. Then a clean man must take some hyssop, dip it in the water, and sprinkle not only the tent of the unclean person but also everything inside it, any people there, and the person who has touched a dead body. After being sprinkled on the seventh day, the unclean person must wash their clothes and take a bath. When evening comes, they will be clean. If they are not purified with water, they will be cut off from Israel.

The man who sprinkles the water must wash his clothes, and anyone who touches the purification water must wash their clothes. They will be unclean until evening. Anything they touch while they are unclean will also be unclean until evening."

Discussion:

What three things were burned with the red cow? Where else have we seen these things?

What do the third day and the seventh day mean to you?

Part II: Numbers 20:1-29

NT: John 4:3-30; Hebrews 6:5-7

The Israelites arrived at the Desert of Zin in the first month. Miriam died there and was buried in Kadesh.

There was no water, and the people were thirsty. They griped at Moses and said, "We should have died when YHVH killed our brothers! Why did you bring us out of Egypt into this terrible place? There is no fruit to eat, and there is not even water to drink!"

Moses and Aaron fell on their faces. The glory of YHVH appeared to them, and YHVH spoke to Moses. He said, "Take the staff. Speak to that rock that is in front of the people, and it will pour out enough water for all the people and animals to drink."

Moses took the budded staff, and he and Aaron gathered the people. Moses said, "Listen, you rebels, must we bring water from this rock?" Moses hit the rock. Water poured out, and everyone drank.

YHVH said to Moses, "Because you hit the rock when I told you to speak to it, because you did not trust Me enough to honor Me in front of the Israelites, you will not bring the people into the Promised Land."

The waters were called *Meribah*, which means "quarreling," because the people complained when they were thirsty.

Soon the Israelites wanted to go through land that was ruled by the king of Edom. Messengers from Moses said, "King of Edom, this is a message from your brother, Israel: You know that the Egyptians made us slaves and mistreated us, but YHVH rescued us and brought us out of Egypt. Now we are camped at Kadesh. Please let us pass carefully through Edom. We will not eat or drink from your land."

The king of Edom said, "If you pass through, we will attack you."

The Israelites asked again, and they offered to pay for food and water, but Edom would not let them pass. The army of Edom attacked the Israelites, and the Israelites went another way.

From Kadesh, the Israelites traveled to Mount Hor, which is also near Edom. YHVH talked with Moses and Aaron. He said, "Because the rock was hit, Aaron will not enter the Promised Land either. Take Aaron and his son Eleazar, and climb Mount Hor. Put Aaron's priestly clothes on Eleazar because Aaron will die on the mountain."

When Moses and Eleazar came down the mountain without Aaron, all the Israelites mourned for thirty days.

Discussion:

Do you think YHVH was angry that the people were thirsty?

What was Moses supposed to do to the rock this second time?

Why do you think the king of Edom refused to let the Israelites pass?

What was Eleazar now that Aaron had died?

Part III: Numbers 21:1-35

NT: John 3:9-21, 12:27-36

The Canaanite king of Arad attacked the Israelites as they traveled down the road to Atharim, and some of the Israelites were captured. Israel promised YHVH, "If You let us defeat this people, we will completely destroy their cities. We will not keep anything that is theirs." YHVH listened, and the Israelites completely destroyed Arad. The place was named *Hormah*, which means "destruction."

The Israelites left Mount Hor and traveled along the Red Sea around Edom. The people were tired and impatient, and they complained to God and Moses. "There is no bread! There is no water! We are sick and tired of manna!"

YHVH sent poisonous snakes to bite the people, and many Israelites died. The people begged Moses to pray for them, and he did. YHVH answered Moses. He told him to make a bronze snake and to lift the snake up on a pole. Anyone who was bitten could look at the snake and live.

The next place the Israelites camped was at Oboth. They moved from Oboth to Iye Abarim (which faces Moab). Then they moved to the Zered Valley. After that, they camped along the Arnon, which is in the wilderness that leads to Amorite territory. The Arnon forms a border between Moab and the Amorites.

Next, the Israelites moved to Beer which is the place where YHVH said, "Gather the people, and I will give them water."

Israel sang, "Spring up, O well! Sing about it, about the well that the princes dug."

After that, the Israelites moved to Mattahan, then to Nahaliel, then to Bamoth, then to the valley of Moab.

The Israelites sent messengers to Sihon, king of the Amorites, because they wanted to pass through his land. They promised not to eat or drink from his land, but Sihon refused just like Edom had done.

Sihon attacked Israel, but the Israelites defeated the Amorites and took over the land from the Arnon to the Jabbok. They did not capture the land of the Ammonites because the

Ammonites had walled cities. Then Israel lived in the cities of the Ammorites— including Heshbon where the king had lived.

The Israelite army went up the road toward Bashan. King Og marched his army to defeat the Israelites, but YHVH was with the Israelites. The Israelites also defeated Og, king of Bashan.

The Israelites traveled to the plains of Moab, and they camped along the Jordan River across from Jericho.

Discussion:

Why did the Israelites vow to YHVV that they would completely destroy their enemies' cities?

What did Yeshua become for us as He was crucified? Does this relate to the snake on the pole?

How does God feel about complaining?

How close are the Israelites to the Promised Land at this point in our reading?

Part IV: Numbers 22:1-41

NT: Jude 11; I Timothy 6:7-10

Balak, Zippor's son, was the king of the Moabites. He was terrified of the Israelites because of what they had done to the Amorites. Because there were so many Israelites, Balak was afraid that Israel would use up all the grass, water, and animals around them. Balak warned the leaders of Midian about this problem.

Near the Euphrates River, there lived a prophet who used his gift to make money. His name was Balaam. The leaders of Moab and Midian took money to Balaam, and Balak sent them with a message: "The Israelites have come out of Egypt, and now they live next to me. Come and put a curse on them so that I can destroy them. Whoever you bless is blessed. Whoever you curse is cursed."

Balaam said, "Stay the night, and I will see what YHVH says about this."

God told Balaam not to go with the men. He said, "You may not curse My blessed people." Balaam sent the men away.

Balak was determined to curse Israel. This time he sent many more impressive men to Balaam. They told Balaam, "Balak says not to let anything stop you from coming. He says you will be rich if you come and curse Israel for him."

Balaam answered, "Even if Balak gave me all his gold and silver, I still could not disobey the command of YHVH my God. Spend the night, and I'll see if YHVH has anything new to say."

God said to Balaam, "Go with the men, but only do what I tell you."

Early the next morning, Balaam got on his donkey and went with the Moabites. God was very angry that he had gone with them. The Angel of YHVH stood in Balaam's way, and the Angel was ready to kill him with a sword. When Balaam's donkey saw the Angel, the donkey turned off the road into a field. Balaam could not see the Angel, and Balaam hit the donkey until it turned back onto the road.

Next, the Angel stood in a narrow path with walls on both sides. When the donkey saw the Angel, it pressed itself against the wall crushing Balaam's foot. Balaam still could not see the Angel, and he hit the donkey again.

Then the Angel stood in a very narrow place where there was no room to move out of the way. When the donkey saw the

Angel, he lay down under Balaam. Balaam was angry, and he hit the donkey again.

YHVH allowed the donkey to speak. It said, "Why have you beat me three times?"

Balaam said, "You're making me look like a fool! I wish I had a sword to kill you with right now!"

The donkey responded and asked, "Have I ever done anything like this before?"

"No," Balaam answered. Then YHVH let Balaam see the Angel who was standing in the road with His sword. Balaam bowed low and fell on his face.

The Angel said to Balaam, "Why have you hit your donkey three times? I came to kill you, and your donkey saved your life."

"I did not realize," Balaam said. "I will turn back if you want."

"Go with them," the Angel said, "but only speak what I tell you to."

When Balaam arrived in Moab, Balak said, "Why did you not come sooner? Don't you know how much I can pay you?"

"I have come now," answered Balaam, "but I can only speak what God lets me say."

The next morning, Balak took Balaam to Bamoth Baal so he could see the border of the Israelite camp.

Discussion:

Why do you think that God told Balaam to go when he asked the second time? Did God change his mind?

Why was God angry that Balaam went with the men after He told him he could? Have your parents ever given you the choice to do something they knew you wanted to do even though they hoped you'd choose wisely?

Part V: Numbers 23:1-25:9

NT: II Peter 2:10-16; Revelation 2:14-15

Balaam told Balak to build him seven altars and to prepare a bull and a ram for each altar. They sacrificed the animals on the altars. Then Balaam told Balak to wait for him while he went to talk to YHVH.

When Balaam returned to Balak and the Moabite leaders, he said the words that YHVH had put in his mouth. Balaam said, "Balak brought me here to curse Jacob. But how can I curse a blessed people? From this mountain, I see a people who live set apart lives and do not think of themselves as members of this world. Who can even count Israel? There are so many of them! Let me die a righteous death and end up like one of them."

Balak was angry, but Balaam reminded him, "I can only speak what YHVH says."

Then Balak took Balaam to another place where he could see the edge of the Israelite camp. Again, Balak built seven altars and sacrificed a bull and a ram on each altar.

Balaam walked away to talk to YHVH. When he came back, he said the words that YHVH had put in his mouth. He said, "Listen, Balak, God doesn't lie or change His mind. He has blessed Israel, and I cannot change that.

God is with Israel, and no harm will come to them. There is no power against them. Israel is like a lion that rises to devour its prey."

Balak said, "If you're not going to curse them, at least don't bless them!"

Balaam replied, "Didn't I tell you that I *have* to do what He tells me to do."

Then Balak took Balaam to another place where they could see the wasteland. He hoped that Balaam would be able to curse Israel from there. As Balaam asked, Balak built seven more altars and sacrificed a bull and a ram on each altar.

Now Balaam could see that YHVH wanted to bless Israel, so he didn't try to make God change His mind. Balaam turned toward the wilderness, and the Spirit of God rested on him. Through the Spirit, Balaam said, "My eyes are opened. I hear God's words, and I bow before Him: How beautiful are your tents, Jacob! They spread out like plants being watered by YHVH. Water will flow from them to their children.

Israel's king will be greater than Agag. God brought Israel out of Egypt, and they are strong. They defeat anyone who is against them. May those YHVH blesses be blessed, and may those He curses be cursed."

Balak was very angry. He tried to send Balaam home, but Balaam continued speaking about what would happen to Balak's people. Balaam said, "A ruler will come out of Israel and will crush Moab, Sheth, Edom, and Seir. All of Israel's enemies will be defeated, and Israel will grow strong. The Amalekites will be completely destroyed. The Kenites will be destroyed. Those who come in to try to conquer will be destroyed as well."

Then Balaam was done speaking, and he went back home.

While Israel camped in Shittim, the Moabite women flirted with the Israelite men, and the Israelite men had relationships with these pagan women. The men ate meat sacrificed to Baal of Peor, the Moabite's god, so they made a covenant with a false god. YHVH was very angry with them. He said to Moses, "Kill all of these people, and I will not be angry with Israel anymore."

Moses told the judges to kill every man who had made a covenant with Baal of Peor. Then, while all of Israel was standing at the door of the Tabernacle and weeping, an Israelite man brought a Moabite woman into the camp—in front of everyone. Pinchas, son of Eleazar and grandson of Aaron, saw this. Pinchas followed the couple into the tent where he killed them both with a sword. This stopped the plague that came from the anger of YHVH, but 24,000 Israelites had already died.

Discussion:

Do you think Balaam wanted to curse Israel? Why didn't Balak give up?

How does God feel about His people being drawn away from Him and His ways?

Why did the Moabite women flirt with the Israelite men?

Pinchas (Phinehas) –
Numbers 25:10 - 30:1; I Kings 18:46 - 19:21; Jeremiah 1:1 - 2:3

Portion:

Part I: Numbers 25:10-18

NT: II Corinthians 6:11-18; John 2:13-17

YHVH said to Moses, "Phineas stopped My anger. Because he cares about holiness and My Name in Israel as much as I do, I am making a covenant of peace with him. The priesthood will stay with him and his sons."

The man Phineas killed was named Zimri. He was the son of Salu, a leader in the Simeonite tribe. The woman's name was Kozbi, she was the daughter of a Midianite chief.

YHVH said, "Because the Midianites tried to trick the Israelites by sending in the chief's daughter, Kozbi, you should treat the Midianites as enemies."

Discussion:

What do you think the Midianites were hoping would happen as a result of Kozbi and Zimri's relationship?

Why did God not want the Israelites to marry the pagan women?

Part II: Numbers 26:1-65

NT: Matthew 18:2-4

After the death of the 24,000, YHVH told Moses to count the fighting men of Israel. Just like before, Moses was told to count all the men over twenty years old who were able to serve in the army.

These are the men Moses counted as Israel camped by the Jordan River across from Jericho:

43,730 from Reuben: including the Hanokite, Palluite, Hezeronite, and Karmite families. Dathan and Abirim, the men who rebelled against Moses, were from the Palluite family.

22,200 from Simeon: including the Nemuelite, Jaminite, Jakinite, Zerahite, and Shaulite families.

40,500 from Gad: including the Zephonite, Haggite, Shunite, Oznite, Erite, Arodite, and Arelite families.

76,500 from Judah: including the Shelanite, Zerahite, and Perezite families. Also counted with Judah were the Hezronite and Hamulite families who were children of Perez. Er and Onan were also sons of Judah, but they died in Canaan.

64,300 from Issachar: including the Tolaite, Puite, Jashubite, and Shimronite families.

60,500 from Zebulun: including the Seredite, Elonite, and Jahleelite families.

52,700 from Joseph's son Manasseh: including the Makirite and Gileadite families. From the Gileadite family came the Iezerite, Helekite, Asrielite, Shechemite, and Hepherite families. Zelophehad was the son of Hepher. Zelophehad had five daughters and no sons.

32,500 from Joseph's son Ephraim: including the Shuthelahite, Bekerite, and Tahanite families. The Eranites were descendants of Shuthelah.

45,600 from Benjamin: including the Belaite, Ashbelite, Ahiramite, Shuphamite, and Huphamite families. The descendants of Bela are the Ardites and the Naamites.

64,400 from Dan: all from Shuhamite families.

53,400 from Asher: including the Imnite, Ishvite, and Beriite families. Through Beriah, the father of the Beriites, also came the Heberite and Malkielite families.

45,400 from Naphtali: including the Jahzeelite, Gunite, Jezerite, and Shillemite families.

All in all, there were 601,730 fighting men in Israel.

YHVH commanded Moses to give the people land as their inheritance. Larger tribes received a larger piece of land, and smaller tribes received a smaller piece of land.

The Levites were not counted with the others because YHVH is their inheritance. He told them that they would not receive land as an inheritance. The families of the Levites were the Gershonites, the Kohathites, the Merarites, the Libnites, the Hebronites, the Mahlites, the Mushites, and the Korahites. Kohath was the father of Amram. Amram married Jochebed, and they had three children: Aaron, Miriam, and Moses. When Moses counted the Levites as they camped beside the Jordan, there were 23,000 Levite males who were over one month old.

No one who was counted that day had been counted in the census at Sinai except for Joshua and Caleb. Everyone else had already died in the wilderness.

Discussion:

When it was time to enter the Promised Land and receive land as an inheritance, which tribe was the largest? Which were the smallest?

What Levite family did Moses and his siblings belong to?

Part III: Numbers 27:1-23

NT: Matthew 25:33-34

A man named Zelophehad belonged to the tribe of Manasseh. He had five daughters and no sons, and he died in the wilderness like the rest of his generation. His daughters were Mahlah, Noah, Hoglah, Milkah, and Tirzah. They came to Moses and said, "Our father had no sons, and now he will not be remembered. Please give us his land inheritance so we can carry on his name."

Moses asked YHVH what he should do, and YHVH answered: "The daughters are right. Give them their father's inheritance. When a man dies without having sons, give his inheritance to his daughters. If he doesn't have daughters, give it to his brothers. If he doesn't have brothers, give it to his father's brothers. If he doesn't have uncles, give it to the closest relative you can find."

Then YHVH told Moses, "Climb this mountain, and look at the Promised Land before you die."

Moses said, "YHVH, please call someone to lead the Israelites after I am gone. They need a shepherd."

YHVH answered, "Joshua, son of Nun, is a leader. Have him stand in front of Eleazar the priest. In front of the Israelites, give him some of your authority so the people will listen to him. If Joshua needs to make a decision, he will go to Eleazar who will get an answer from YHVH. Joshua will command the people, and they will obey him."

Moses obeyed YHVH.

Discussion:

Why did Zelophehad's daughters ask Moses for their father's inheritance?

Why was it important for Moses to make Joshua the leader while he was still alive?

Part IV: Numbers 28:1-31

NT: Luke 22:1-20

YHVH commanded Moses to teach the Israelites about the offerings. YHVH said, "Every day, once in the morning and again in the evening, they must bring food offerings to Me. What I want for this food offering is one lamb burned on the altar with a grain offering of fine flour and olive oil. A drink offering of wine should be poured on the ground for Me."

On the Sabbath day, I want you to bring Me two more lambs. Also bring these lambs with a grain offering and a drink offering.

At the beginning of every month, bring Me a burned offering of two young bulls, one ram, and seven perfect one-year-old lambs as a food offering. Each animal should be offered with a grain offering mixed with olive oil as well as a drink offering poured on the ground for Me. These offerings should be made at the new moon for each month. With this food offering, also bring one male goat as a purification offering."

YHVH said, "The fourteenth day of the first month is YHVH's Passover. Starting on the fifteenth day, you must eat unleavened bread for seven days. The first day is a day of rest.

With the regular offerings, also bring this offering every day for the seven days: a food offering of two young bulls, one ram, and seven perfect one-year-old lambs. Each animal should be offered with a fine grain offering mixed with olive oil. Also offer one male goat for purification. The seventh day of the feast is another day of rest."

YHVH said, "When you present new grain to YHVH on the day of first fruits, everyone should come together and rest. On this day, along with the regular offerings, also give YHVH a food offering of two young bulls, one ram, and seven perfect one-year-old lambs. Each animal should be offered with a fine grain offering mixed with olive oil. Also offer one male goat for purification."

Discussion:

On what days did YHVH ask for more than just the regular food offerings?

Part V: Numbers 29:1-30:1

NT: Philippians 2:14-18

YHVH said, "The first day of the seventh month is a day for you to blow the trumpets. It is a day of rest. On this day, along with the regular daily offerings and the new month offering, give YHVH a food offering of two young bulls, one ram, and seven perfect one-year-old lambs. Each animal should be offered with a drink offering and a fine grain offering mixed with olive oil. Also offer one male goat for purification."

YHVH commanded, "Gather together on the tenth day of the seventh month for a day of rest and fasting. With the regular offerings, give YHVH a food offering of two young bulls, one ram, and seven perfect one-year-old lambs. Each animal should be offered with a drink offering and a fine grain offering mixed with olive oil. Also offer one male goat for purification.

Gather together on the fifteenth day of the seventh month for a day of rest. Celebrate a feast to YHVH for seven days. With the regular offerings, this is what you should give to YHVH on each day of the feast:

On the first day, offer thirteen young bulls, two rams, and fourteen perfect one-year-old lambs. Offer each animal with a grain offering and drink offering. Also offer one male goat for purification.

On the second day, offer twelve young bulls, two rams, and fourteen perfect one-year-old lambs. Offer each animal with a grain offering and drink offering. Also offer one male goat for purification.

On the third day, offer eleven young bulls, two rams, and fourteen perfect one-year-old lambs. Offer each animal with a grain offering and drink offering. Also offer one male goat for purification.

On the fourth day, offer ten young bulls, two rams, and fourteen perfect one-year-old lambs. Offer each animal with a grain offering and drink offering. Also offer one male goat for purification.

On the fifth day, offer nine young bulls, two rams, and fourteen perfect one-year-old lambs. Offer each animal with a grain offering and drink offering. Also offer one male goat for purification.

On the sixth day, offer eight young bulls, two rams, and fourteen perfect one-year-old lambs. Offer each animal with a grain offering and drink offering. Also offer one male goat for purification.

On the seventh day, offer seven young bulls, two rams, and fourteen perfect one-year-old lambs. Offer each animal with a grain offering and drink offering. Also offer one male goat for purification.

On the eighth day, the people should gather for a day of rest. Offer one bull, one ram, and seven perfect one-year-old lambs. Offer each animal with a grain offering and drink offering. Also offer one male goat for purification.

You should offer all these things, as well as any extra offerings you want to bring, to YHVH."

So Moses taught the Israelites about the offerings.

Discussion:

What do these daily and feast offerings remind you of? Do you eat special meals on special days?

Mattot (Tribes) –
Numbers 30:2 - 32:42; Jeremiah 1:1 - 2:3

Massei (Stages) –
Numbers 33:1 - 36:13;
Jeremiah 2:4-28, 3:4, 4:1-2

(In leap years these portions are read separately.)

Portion:

Part I: Numbers 30:1-31:54

NT: Matthew 5:33-37

Moses said to the leaders of Israel, "This is what YHVH commands: If a man makes a vow to YHVH, he must do everything he said he would do. If a girl makes a vow to YHVH while she is still in her father's house, then her father may undo the vow if he wants to. If her father does not undo the vow as soon as he hears about it, she must do everything she said she would do. The same rule applies for a woman who has a husband; her husband may also undo the vow she made. If her husband does not undo the vow as soon as he hears about it, she must do everything she said she would do. If a divorced woman or a widow makes a vow to YHVH, she must do everything she said she would do."

Then YHVH said to Moses, "Defeat the Midianites because of what they did to Israel." So Moses sent 1,000 men from each tribe into battle against the Midianites. He sent Phineas, the son of Eleazar the priest, with the holy things and trumpets. The Israelites killed all the Midianite men including the leaders of Midian. They also found Balaam and killed him. They took the women and children alive. They took all their things and livestock, but they burned the cities to the ground.

When Moses saw that they had not killed the women, he was very angry. These were the same women who followed Balaam's advice and flirted with the men of Israel causing the men to sin against YHVH. This had made YHVH angry, and He'd sent a plague to the Israelites. Moses said, "You must only allow the young girls to live. Every woman who has been with a man must die, and every male Midianite must die. The girls may be maidservants or marry Israelite men."

Then he said, "Everyone who has been in battle must stay outside the camp for seven days. Each one must be purified on the third day and again on the seventh day. Also, clean everything you've taken from the Midianites. Clean every piece of clothing and every object. Every metal object should be cleaned with fire and water. Everything else should be cleaned with water only. Clean your clothes on the seventh day before coming back into the camp.

Count up everything that was taken from the Midianites and divide it into two equal halves. One half belongs to the men who went to battle, and the other half belongs to the rest of Israel. From the half that belongs to the fighting men, take one of every 500th maidservant, cattle, donkey, and sheep and give them to Eleazar the priest. He will dedicate them to YHVH. From Israel's half, take one of every fiftieth and give them to the Levites."

Everything was divided as YHVH commanded. Then the men who went to battle came to Moses and said, "We have counted, and not even one of us died in battle." The men then brought an offering to YHVH. To give thanks and to repay for their lives, they gave YHVH the gold jewelry they had found. Moses and Eleazar collected the gold from the men, and they presented it to YHVH. Four hundred and twenty pounds of gold were collected from the men and placed in the Tabernacle as a reminder of what YHVH did when none of the Israelites died in battle against the Midianites.

Discussion:

What is something someone might vow to YHVH?

Why do you think the boys were not allowed to live but the girls were?

Part II: Numbers 32:1-42

NT: Matthew 4:24-25

The tribes of Reuben and Gad both had a lot of livestock, and they needed good grazing land. They saw that the land around them was good for grazing. They asked Moses, "Could we live in this land instead of crossing over the Jordan to the Promised Land?"

Moses answered, "Why would you want to discourage your brothers from crossing the Jordan River? Should they have to fight for the land without your help? Remember how scared your fathers were when they had their chance to enter the Promised Land? Are you going to act like they did when they made God angry? He made them wander for forty years until they had all died in the wilderness!"

The men answered and said, "Just allow us to build pens for our animals and homes for our children. Then we will cross the Jordan with our brothers, and we will fight for the land with them. We will not return home until all our brothers have received their inheritance in Canaan. We know we will not have an inheritance in the land, because we have already claimed our land on this side of the river."

Moses agreed. He told the rest of the Israelites, "If your brothers from Reuben and Gad enter the land armed for battle, and if they fight for you, you should give them the land on this side of the Jordan. If they do not keep their word and enter the land to fight for you, they will have to claim their inheritance in Canaan, too."

The men from Gad and Reuben agreed. Moses gave to the tribes of Reuben, Gad, and the half-tribe of Manasseh the land that had belonged to the Amorites and King Og of Bashan, and they built cities there.

Discussion:

Why do you think these tribes did not want to live in the land YHVH had promised?

Part III: Numbers 33:1-56

NT: Acts 7

This is the history of the Israelites' time in the wilderness: The Israelites left Rameses on the fifteenth day of the first month: the day after the Passover. They marched out of Egypt in front of all the Egyptians while the Egyptians were burying their sons.

First, the Israelites camped in Succoth. After Succoth, they camped in Etham on the edge of the wilderness. Next, they camped in Pihahiroth in front of Migdol. They went through the sea and walked three days in the wilderness of Etham until they camped in Marah. Next, they came to Elim where there were twelve fountains of water and seventy palm trees. When they left Elim, they camped by the Red Sea.

After the Red Sea, they camped in the wilderness of Sin. Next, they camped in Dophkah, and after Dophkah in Alush. After Alush, they camped in Rephidim where there was no water for the people. When they left Rephidim, they traveled to the wilderness of Sinai.

When they left the Sinai, they went to Kibrothhataavah. Afterward, they camped at Hazeroth. After Hazeroth, they camped in Rithmah. When they left there, they camped at

Rimmonparez and afterward in Libnah. When they left Libnah, they camped at Rissah and then in Kehelathah. Next, they camped near Mount Shapher, and then they went to Haradah. When they left Haradah, they camped in Makheloth.

After Makheloth, the Israelites camped at Talath and then at Tarah. Next, they went to Mithcah and then to Hashmonah. After Hashmonah, the Israelites moved from Moseroth to Benejaakan to Horhagidgad to Jotbathah. After Jotbathah, they traveled to Ebronah and then to Eziongaber.

Next, the Israelites camped in the wilderness of Zin (which is Kadesh). After Kadesh, they camped near Mount Hor on the edge of the land of Edom. God told Aaron, the high priest, to climb Mount Hor, and Aaron died there. Aaron died on the first day of the fifth month of Israel's fortieth year in the wilderness. Aaron was one hundred and twenty-three years old when he died.

King Arad, the Canaanite, heard that the Israelites were coming. When they left Mount Hor, they went to Zalmonah and then to Punon. From Punon, they went to Oboth. Next, they went to Ijeabarim which is on the border of Moab. They traveled to Dibongad and camped in Almondiblathaim. Next, they camped in the mountains of Abarim (before Nebo). After leaving Abarim, Israel camped by the Jordan across from Jericho.

While they were in the plains near Jericho, YHVH gave Moses a message for the people. He said, "Tell them that when they cross the Jordan they must drive away all the people who live there. Tell them they must destroy all the people's carved idols and metal idols and all their places of worship because the people there do not worship YHVH. Then, you will divide the land by tribe as your inheritance from YHVH. If you do not defeat the people before you take over the land, they will be trouble for you for many years to come. I will do to you what I was going to do to them."

Discussion:

How many stops did the Israelites make in their forty years?

Where did they receive the Law of YHVH?

Where did Aaron die?

Part IV: Numbers 34:1-29

NT: Revelation 21

YHVH said to Moses, "Tell the children of Israel about the land of Canaan. The land is their inheritance. The southern border of Canaan is the wilderness of Zin along the coast of Edom to the outer coast of the Salt Sea. Turning from the south, the border is from Akrabbim on to Zin and from Kadeshbarnea to Hazaraddar to Azmon. From Azmon, the border of Canaan turns to the river of Egypt and ends at the sea.

The great sea is Canaan's border on the west. On the north, the border runs from the great sea to Mount Hor. Then, mark from Mount Hor to the entrance of Hamath and along Hamath to Zedad along to Ziphron and Hazarenan.

Mark the eastern border from Hazarenan to Shepham. The coast extends from Shepham to Riblah (on the east of Ain). From there, the border reaches down the side of the Sea of Chinnereth to the east. The eastern border runs down to Jordan along the Jordan to the Salt Sea."

Moses told the Israelites, "This is the land you should divide among the nine and a half tribes who will inherit the land of Canaan."

YHVH said to Moses, "Eleazar the priest and Joshua son of Nun are the men who will divide the land. One leader from each tribe will also work to divide the land.

From Judah, Caleb son of Jephunneh; from Simeon, Shemuel son of Ammihud; from Benjamin, Elidad son of Chislon; from Dan, Bukki son of Jogli; from Manasseh, Hanniel son of

Ephod; from Ephraim, Kemuel son of Shiphtan; from Zebulun, Elizaphan son of Parnach; from Issachar, Paltiel son of Azzan; from Asher, Ahihud son of Shelomi; from Naphtali, Pedahel son of Ammihud.

Discussion:

Which tribes were going to settle across the Jordan and which were staying behind?

Part V: Numbers 35:1-36:13

NT: I Thessalonians 4:1-7; Revelation 6:9-11

YHVH gave Moses a message for the Israelites. He said, "Make sure the Levites have cities to live in. Each tribe must give the Levites cities. Tribes that have fewer cities will give few, and those that have many cities will give more. All in all, the Levites should be given forty-two cities to live in. Each city given to the Levites must have a thousand cubits of land around the wall and then two thousand cubits of land after that so the Levites will have plenty of land for their livestock. In addition to these forty-two cities, the Levites will be put in charge of six cities of refuge. Three cities of refuge should be built on each side of the Jordan.

If someone kills another person, they may run and hide in the closest city of refuge until the Israelite court decides whether they are guilty of murder. If two or three witnesses saw the guilty person kill the victim on purpose, that guilty person will die. If the witnesses saw that the killing was an accident, the guilty person will be allowed to go back to the city of refuge to live there until the current high priest has died. If the killer leaves the city of refuge before the high priest has died, the avenger of blood will be allowed to kill him.

If someone is sentenced to die, no one may pay money to change the judge's mind. If someone is sentenced to live in a city of refuge, no one may pay money to change the judge's mind. The killer must stay there until the high priest has died. Blood makes the land unholy, and things are only made right by the blood of the killer. Do not make the land unholy because I, YHVH, live there with My people."

Leaders of Gilead from the tribe of Manasseh came to Moses and the leaders with a problem. They said, "You gave Zelophehad's daughters the inheritance that belonged to their father. But now, what if they marry someone from outside their own tribe? If they do, their father's inheritance will be given to their husbands' tribe, and it will be taken away from us."

Moses heard from YHVH. Then he answered, "Yes, this is a concern. If an inheritance is given to a daughter, she must marry within her own tribe so that the inheritance will not pass from one tribe to another. The daughters of Zelophehad may marry whomever they choose from their own tribe." So the daughters of Zelophehad married their father's brother's sons.

These are the commands that YHVH spoke through Moses while the people were camped across the river from Jericho.

Discussion:

What is the purpose of a city of refuge?

Who is the avenger of blood?

What were the men from the five sisters' tribe concerned about losing?

Devarim (Words) – Deuteronomy 1:1 - 3:22; Isaiah 1:1-27

Portion:

Part I: Deuteronomy 1:1-18

NT: II Corinthians 1:20

Israel was still camped on the east of the Jordan River. (It's an eleven-day trip from Horeb to Kadesh Barnea if you take the Mount Seir road.) On the first day of the eleventh month, in their fortieth year of wandering in the wilderness, Moses reminded the Israelites of everything they'd been through.

After they had defeated Sihon, king of the Amorites, and Og, king of Bashan, Moses said, "While we were camped at Horeb, YHVH told us that it was time to move and to take the land of the Amorites and Canaanites. He said He had given us the land, all the way to the Euphrates, because that is the same land He promised to Abraham, Isaac, and Jacob.

At that same time, I was tired of leading all of you. It was too much work for one man. I asked you to pick wise men from each tribe, and I made them leaders to help me in my work. These men handled the smaller arguments and problems that you had with one another, and they only brought the difficult cases to me. I told these judges, "Be fair in all your decisions—no matter who you are judging."

Discussion:

What point in time is Moses reminding the people of?

How far are they from Canaan?

Part II: Deuteronomy 1:19-46

NT: Matthew 21:18-22; Hebrews 3:7-4:11

"As YHVH commanded, we left Horeb and traveled toward the country of the Amorites. When we reached Kadesh Barnea, I told you that it was time to take the land. 'Do not be afraid,' I said. Then you said that you would like to send spies to explore the land first. This seemed like a good idea to me, so I chose one man from each tribe. These twelve men went in and explored the land of Canaan, and they saw that it was a very good land. However, ten of the spies told scary stories about giant people who lived there. The stories scared you, and you were afraid to go and take the land that YHVH had promised to give you. Even though you had seen YHVH do many, many miracles, you still did not trust Him. You were afraid you were going to die.

YHVH heard you, and He became very angry. He said that none of you would ever see the Promised Land—that only your children would see it. Because Joshua and Caleb were the only two spies who had encouraged the people to have faith, God made an exception for them. They would be the only Israelite adults not to die in the wilderness. The children of the fearful Israelites would grow up in the wilderness, and they would enter the land later with Joshua and Caleb. YHVH was also angry at me, and He said that I could not enter the Promised Land either. He told me that Joshua would lead the people after I died.

YHVH told us to turn around and to head back to the desert, but you decided to go to the Promised Land instead. You said, 'We have sinned, and we want to make things right. We are ready to obey now!' I warned you that it was too late. I told you that YHVH was not with you, but you would not listen to me. You tried to take the land without God's help, and the enemy beat you; they chased you down from Seir all the way to Hormah. You cried loudly to YHVH, but He did not listen to you."

Discussion:

YHVH gave Israel the land of Canaan. Could they take it without His help? Are there right ways and wrong ways to accept God's promises?

Part III: Deuteronomy 2:1-23

NT: Romans 8:31-32

"Because YHVH told us to, we walked through the wilderness toward the Red Sea, and we wandered around in the country of Seir. After a long time in that land, YHVH told us to go north. He said, 'You are about to pass through land that belongs to the children of Esau. Do not make them angry or fight with them. Pay them for anything you eat or drink. I will not give their land to you because I promised it to Esau.' (There had been a strong and tall people living in that land, but the descendants of Esau chased them away.)

After we passed our relatives from Esau, we traveled along the desert road which belonged to the people of Moab. YHVH said, 'Do not fight with the Moabites. They are children of Lot, and I gave the land of Ar to him.' (There had been a strong and tall people living in the land of Moab, but the descendants of Lot chased them away.)

After thirty-eight years of wandering, YHVH led us across the Zered Valley. By that time, every last man counted in the first census had died. That was the generation that was counted before the ten spies brought bad news and before the people became afraid and made God angry. YHVH led us past Lot's inheritance in the land of Ar. He said, 'Do not bother the Ammonites or try to take their land. This is the land I gave to their father, Lot.' The Ammonites and the Moabites are both descendants of Lot. YHVH was also with the Ammonites, and they chased giants from their land as well."

Discussion:

Why was it important for Moses to remind the Israelites about the land promised to Esau and Lot and about the giants that had lived in their land?

Part IV: Deuteronomy 2:24-37

NT: II Thessalonians 3:1-3

Moses continued: "Then YHVH said, 'Cross the Arnon. I have given you the land of Sihon, king of the Amorites. Begin to take it. Today, I have made everyone terrified of you.'

I sent peaceful messages to Sihon, and I asked if we could walk through his land. I told him we would buy what we ate and drank. But YHVH gave Sihon a stubborn heart so that we could go to battle and defeat the Amorites. Sihon refused to let us walk through his land, and he brought his army to attack us. We left no survivors in our battle with the Amorites, but we took their things and their livestock for ourselves. Not one of Sihon's towns was too strong for us. We defeated them all. But we obeyed YHVH, and we did not try to take any land from the Ammonites."

Discussion:

Why did Moses send a message to Sihon?

Part V: Deuteronomy 3:1-22

NT: Luke 1:68-75

"Next, we defeated King Og, the Amorite king of the land of Bashan. YHVH said, 'Do to Og what you did to Sihon.' So we took all of Og's sixty cities as well as his villages. The cities had high walls and strong gates, but we took them all and left no survivors. Og was the last of the Rephaite giants, and his bed was over fourteen feet long.

From these two kings of the Amorites, we took the land east of the Jordan from Arnon to Mount Hermon. We took all the towns and all of Gilead. We took all of Bashan to the edge of Og's kingdom.

I gave this land north of Aroer to the Reubenites and Gadites. The rest of Gilead, and all of Bashan, I gave to the half-tribe of Manasseh. I told the fighting men of Ruben, Gad, and Manasseh that they would have to leave their women, children, and livestock in the safety of the towns they built. They must go with the rest of you, across the Jordan, to fight for the Promised Land. When all the Israelites have received their inheritance of land, they will be allowed to go back to their families and towns.

Then I said to Joshua, 'You can see what YHVH has done to these two kings. He will do the same thing in all the kingdoms where you are going. Do not be afraid. YHVH is with you.' "

Discussion:

Do you think that the Israelites did not know about these things that had happened in the last forty years? Why was it so important for Moses to remind them of their sins and victories?

Va'etchanan (I pleaded) –
Deuteronomy 3:23 - 7:11; Isaiah 40:1-26

Portion:

Part I: Deuteronomy 3:23-4:14

NT: Acts 13:13-43

Moses said, "After encouraging Joshua and reminding him of all YHVH has done for us, I pleaded with God. I asked Him to please let me go in and see the Promised Land. He was angry with me because of you, and He told me not to ask Him again. He told me to go up to the top of Pisgah and to look all around at the land below. Since I would not be allowed to step foot in the land, I was allowed to see it from there.

Now, listen to me as I teach you. Do not add or take away from these laws, but follow them exactly so that you will be blessed in the land. Don't forget what happened to the Israelites who followed Baal of Peor. You are alive because you were faithful to God.

I have taught you as YHVH commanded. Follow these instructions. If you do, the nations around you will see that you are wise. No other nation has their gods near them, but YHVH is close to us when we pray. He gives us fair laws that are good for our lives.

Do not forget the things you have seen YHVH do. Teach your children about them. Remember the day you heard YHVH speaking to you through fire and smoke from the mountain. He gave you His covenant: the Ten Commandments. And He gave me the laws for the Promised Land so that I could teach you how to live there."

Discussion:

What happened to the Israelites that followed Baal of Peor?

Why was Moses not allowed to go into the Promised Land?

Part II: Deuteronomy 4:15-43

NT: John 7:35; James 1:1

Moses said, "You did not see YHVH on the mountain; you only heard Him. Do not try to make any images of God—no matter what that image looks like. And when you look into the sky and see the sun, moon, and stars, do not be tempted to worship them. YHVH is the One who rescued you from Egypt and made you His people.

Because of you, I will die in this land. But you are about to enter the good land. Do not forget the covenant you have with YHVH. Do not make any idols. He is a jealous God and a burning fire.

After you have lived in the land a long time and have had many children and grandchildren, if you begin to forget God, and if you turn to some kind of idol, I call Heaven and Earth to witness against you. You will quickly be destroyed, and the few who live will be forced to leave the land. YHVH will make you live with pagan people. You will worship gods made of wood and stone. But then, if you begin to seek YHVH again, if you turn back to Him and obey Him, He will not leave you helpless. He will remember the covenant He made with your fathers.

In all of time, from the very beginning, has anything ever happened that is as wonderful as what's happened to you? Has God chosen and rescued any other nation? Has anyone else heard God speak to them through fire and lived to tell about it? You have seen the wonderful things of YHVH so that you will know He is the only God. Because He loved your ancestors, He has brought you here. He will chase mighty nations out of the land that He promised to give to your fathers.

Let your hearts say that there is no other God but YHVH. Keep His commands which I am giving you today. If you do this, you and your children will be blessed in the land."

After this, Moses chose three cities on the east side of the Jordan. He made them cities of refuge. YHVH had commanded the Israelites to have cities of refuge. If someone killed someone accidentally, they could run there and stay safe. East of the Jordan, there was a city for the Reubenites, a city for the Gadites, and a city for the Manassites.

Discussion:

What will the nations think when they see Israel following YHVH's laws?

People are tempted to make an image for God so they can see what they are worshipping. What does YHVH say about this?

Part III: Deuteronomy 4:44-5:33

NT: John 14:15-31; Romans 7:7-25

These are the laws Moses gave to the Israelites after they defeated kings Og and Sihon and lived in that land on the east of the Jordan:

"Listen to these laws, Israel. When YHVH made a covenant with us at Horeb, it was not a covenant with our ancestors. It was with all of us who are alive here today. He spoke from the mountain and said,

'I am YHVH your God who rescued you from slavery.

Have no other gods but Me.

Do not make any idols.

Do not misuse My name.

Keep the Sabbath day: Do not work or require any person or animal to work.

Honor your father and mother and you will have a good, long life.

Do not murder.

Do not commit adultery.

Do not steal.

Do not give a false testimony.

Do not want things that belong to someone else.'

He spoke those words from the mountain. Then He wrote them on two stone tablets that He gave to me.

When you heard His voice from the mountain that was covered with fire, your leaders came to me and said, 'We have learned that people can hear YHVH and live; but if we hear Him any longer, we will die. Go and hear from Him for us. We will do whatever He tells us to do.'

YHVH was happy with what you said, and He gave me the laws to give to you. Now be careful to do whatever YHVH has commanded. Be obedient to Him so you may live long lives and be blessed in the land He is giving you."

Discussion:

When did the people first hear YHVH speak these commands?

Part IV: Deuteronomy 6:1-25

NT: Mark 12:28-34

"These are the laws YHVH commanded me to teach you about living in the Promised Land. Follow them so that you, your children, and your grandchildren will be blessed.

Hear me, people of Israel: YHVH our God, YHVH is one. Love YHVH with all your heart, with all your soul, and with all your strength. These commandments that I am teaching you today should be always on your hearts. Teach them to your children. Talk about them all day long, and apply them to your lives. Tie them as signs on your hands, and write them on your foreheads. Write them on your doorframes and your gates.

YHVH is about to bring you into the Promised Land. It is a good land. You will live in cities that you didn't have to build. You will drink from wells that you didn't have to dig. You will eat from gardens and vineyards that you didn't have to plant. You will be happy and well-fed, but be careful. Remember that YHVH brought you out of slavery. Do not forget Him.

Do not fear anyone but YHVH. Do not test God by following any other gods. Be sure to do whatever YHVH has told you to do so that you may live in the good land.

When your children ask you someday, 'What do all these laws mean, and why do we follow them?' you will tell them that the Israelites were slaves in Egypt. You will tell them how YHVH rescued us from slavery, made us His people, and taught us to live righteous lives in the land He'd promised to our fathers."

Discussion:

Is it easier for us to remember YHVH when things are easy or difficult?

Part V: Deuteronomy 7:1-11

NT: II Corinthians 6:14-18

"When YHVH brings you into the Promised Land and gives you victory over the Hittites, Girgashites, Amorites, Canaanites, Perizzites, Hivites, and Jebusites, be sure to completely destroy them. Do not try to be friends with the pagan nations. Do not allow your sons and daughters to marry their sons and daughters. They will cause you to worship other gods.

Smash all their idols and altars because YHVH has chosen you for Himself—to be *His* special people. YHVH did not decide to love you because you were such a big, mighty nation. You were small. He loved you because He loved you. He loved you because He loved your ancestors, and He made promises to them. He is faithful to those who keep His commandments, but He will destroy those who are against Him."

Discussion:

Why was it not okay to allow the pagan people to live nearby?

Ekev (Because) –
Deuteronomy 7:12 - 11:25; Isaiah 49:14 - 51:3

Portion:

Part I: Deuteronomy 7:12-26

NT: Luke 16:10-15

"If you follow all YHVH's instructions, He will keep His covenant with you just as He promised your ancestors. He will bless your crops and your animals and your families. You will be more blessed than any other nation. You will not be sick with diseases, but the nations who hate you will be.

When YHVH allows you to defeat the enemy nations, you must destroy them. If you don't destroy them, you will end up following their gods. Don't be afraid of the pagan nations that YHVH is giving you to destroy. Do not say, 'These people are stronger than we are!' Remember everything you have seen YHVH do for you. Remember what He did to the Egyptians? He will do the same to these people.

YHVH will not give you victory over all your enemies at once. There are not enough of you to take over the whole land, yet. If He gave you the whole land too soon, the wild animals would take over and surround you. He will give you victory a little at a time. Whenever He gives you an enemy to destroy, they will not be able to fight against you. He will use you to wipe out the pagan kings and their nations. When you see their gold and silver idols, do not be tempted by them. Burn all the idols completely. Do not bring them into your homes, or you will be destroyed."

Discussion:

Why might the Israelites be tempted by the pagan idols?

Israel should already know how God will defeat their enemies. Why?

Part II: Deuteronomy 8:1-20

NT: Matthew 4:1-4

"Keep every command of YHVH so that you may enter the Promised Land and be blessed there. Do not forget your time in the wilderness. YHVH has used this time to teach you. He has humbled you and tested you to see whether you will follow Him or not. He allowed you to go hungry, and then He fed you manna. He wanted you to understand that you cannot live on bread only.

You need Him and the words that He speaks. Your clothes have lasted and your feet have not swelled all this time in the wilderness. Know that YHVH has been with you. He has disciplined you the way a father disciplines a son.

YHVH is bringing you into a good land where you will have plenty to eat and drink. Do not forget Him. Do not forget to obey His commands. If you forget to be thankful to YHVH, you might start to think that you are blessed because of your own work. It is YHVH who will bless you. If you forget YHVH and begin to follow other gods, you will be destroyed just like the other nations that YHVH has destroyed."

Discussion:

What was the purpose of Israel's time in the wilderness?

Have you ever been in a wilderness time where things have been really hard?

Part III: Deuteronomy 9:1-29

NT: Titus 3:3-7

"Understand me, Israel: You are about to cross the Jordan and conquer a nation of giants. You have heard about them, and you have talked about them. You have said, 'Who could ever defeat the giant Anakites?' But you will! YHVH will go ahead of you, and He will use you to destroy them.

Once they are destroyed, do not become prideful. Do not think that YHVH has chosen you because you are so good and so righteous. YHVH has destroyed these nations because of their wickedness—not because of your goodness. You are a stubborn people. YHVH is keeping the promise He made to Abraham, Isaac, and Jacob.

Never forget how angry you have made YHVH. When YHVH called me up the mountain to receive the stone tablets, I was there for forty days and nights without food and water. While I was there, you turned against God. You turned against Him so quickly! YHVH wanted to destroy you. I threw down the tablets and broke them because I was so angry at you.

I fell on my face before YHVH, and I prayed for you for forty days and forty nights. I didn't eat or drink because what you had done was so evil. YHVH was angry, and He wanted to destroy you. I prayed for you. I also prayed for Aaron, because YHVH was angry enough to destroy him, too.

You made God mad at other times. When He was ready to lead you into the Promised Land, you rebelled against Him again. You have been rebellious for as long as I've known you! Again, YHVH wanted to destroy you. Again, I lay on my face for forty days, and I prayed that YHVH wouldn't kill you. I begged Him not to destroy His inheritance. I said, 'Our enemies will think that You don't keep Your promises!' I asked Him to remember Abraham, Isaac, and Jacob."

Discussion:

What is the reason that YHVH destroyed the pagan people and allowed the Israelites to take over the land?

Part IV: Deuteronomy 10:1-22

NT: James 2:1-13

"After I had prayed for you again, YHVH said, 'Cut two more tablets and bring them up here to Me. I will write what I wrote on the stones that you broke. Also make an ark. You will put the new tablets inside it.'

I made an ark, and I cut the new stones just as YHVH had said. He wrote the commandments He had spoken to you through fire: the same ones He had written on the first set of tablets. I was on the mountain for forty days—just like I was the first time. He listened to me; it was not YHVH's will to destroy you. He told me to go back down the mountain and to lead you so that you could enter the Promised Land.

Fear YHVH. Walk in His ways. Everything belongs to YHVH, but He chose your ancestors. He loved them, and He chose you—their children—above all the nations. Circumcise your hearts, and do not be stubborn anymore. Treat the poor and the stranger among you with kindness—as YHVH does. Remember that you were foreigners in Egypt. Serve YHVH who has done many miracles for you. When you went into Egypt, you were a family of only seventy people. Now you are as many as the stars in the sky."

Discussion:

Why does Moses/YHVH continually remind the Israelites that they were slaves in Egypt?

Part V: Deuteronomy 11:1-25

NT: Acts 14:8-18

"Love YHVH your God, and keep all His commandments. Remember that you, not your children, are the ones who saw the miracles of YHVH. You are the ones who saw what He did to the Egyptians. You saw the earth open up to swallow Dathan and Abiram and their families.

Obey all YHVH's commands so you will have the strength to go in and take the Promised Land. It is a good land that is cared for by YHVH Himself. If you are faithful to Him, He promises to send rain at the right times so that your crops will be blessed. But if you turn away from YHVH, if you follow other gods, He will shut up the heavens. There will be no rain, and you will be destroyed.

Remember these words I am telling you. Keep them safe in your hearts and minds. Tie them around your hands, and put them on your foreheads. Teach them to your children when you're at home, when you're out walking, when you wake in the morning, and when you tuck them in at night. Write them on the doorways of your homes and on your gates. If you do, you and your children will live long lives in the Promised Land. You will drive out the other nations. No one will be able to defeat you if you are careful to follow all the commands of YHVH your God."

Discussion:

What comes as a sign of blessing from YHVH?

Re'eh (See) –
Deuteronomy 11:26 - 16:17; Isaiah 54:11 - 55:5

Portion:

Part I: Deuteronomy 11:26-12:32

NT: Luke 11:27-28

"I'm offering you a choice. You can be blessed, or you can be cursed. If you want to be blessed, keep all these commands. If you want to be cursed, follow other gods and disobey the commands of YHVH your God. When you enter the land, climb Mount Gerizim and speak the blessings; climb Mount Ebal and speak the curses.

Be careful not to allow any pagan worship in the land YHVH is giving to you. The nations that live there now have built altars to other gods. Smash and burn every idol and altar that you find. Do not worship YHVH the way the pagans worship their gods. He will show you where you should go to worship. To that place, and only to that place, should you bring your tithes and offerings.

Today, you eat your tithe where you choose; once you enter the land, YHVH will choose a special place for you to worship His Name. You will bring your sacrifices and offerings there, and you will rejoice in the presence of YHVH. You will not burn sacrifices in any other place; you will only offer them in the place that YHVH chooses for His Name.

Once YHVH has given you all the land He's promised, some of you will live far away from the place He has chosen for His Name. You will not want to make the long trip just so that you can eat meat. But if you want to eat meat, you can still eat meat. Kill and eat from your livestock or hunt for your meat; it is a meal, not a sacrifice. Eat as much meat as you want, but pour the blood out on the ground. Do not eat the blood.

If you want to offer an animal to God, you must go to the place that YHVH has chosen. Pour the blood beside the altar, and place the fat on the altar. Then you may eat the parts of the animal that you are allowed to eat.

YHVH will give you victory over the people who live in the land. When the people have been destroyed, do not wonder about how they worshipped their gods. They do horrible things; they even sacrifice their children.

Do everything YHVH has commanded you to do. Do not add to these commands, and do not take away from them."

Discussion:

What is the difference between a meal and a sacrifice?

Why might someone be tempted to worship YHVH in pagan ways?

Part II: Deuteronomy 13:1-18

NT: I John 4:1-6

"If a prophet comes to you and tells you to follow other gods, do not listen to him. Even if all his predictions come true, still do not believe him. God is allowing these prophets to test you. You must follow YHVH. You must put that prophet to death. Even if it is your own friend or close family member who says, 'Let's go worship another god,' that person must be killed.

If you hear that the people in one of your towns have started to worship another god, you must find out if this is true. If it is true, you must kill everyone in that town. Destroy the town, and do not rebuild there. Then, YHVH will have mercy on you. He will bless you because you keep His commands."

Discussion:

Moses warns the people that false prophets will try to talk them into worshipping other gods. What will these false prophets be allowed to do to try to convince the Israelites?

Part III: Deuteronomy 14:1-28

NT: Acts 10

"YHVH has chosen you as His special people. Do not act like the pagans around you. Do not cut yourselves or shave yourselves as a way of mourning for the dead.

Do not eat anything you are not allowed to eat. If an animal has a divided hoof and chews the cud, then you may eat it. If it only has a divided hoof or only chews the cud, it is not clean; it is not food for you.

You may eat any fish that has both fins and scales.

You may eat any clean bird, but you may not eat the birds that scavenge the earth for dead and dying things.

Flying insects are unclean, but you may eat the winged insects that are clean.

Do not eat anything that you found already dead. You may sell or give this food to foreigners, but you may not eat it. You are a set apart people.

Do not cook a young goat in its mother's milk.

Set aside a tenth of all your produce and livestock each year. Eat this tithe in the place that YHVH chooses. If you live too far away from the place that YHVH chooses, you may exchange your tithe for silver and make your journey with the silver instead. Then, when you get to the place YHVH chooses, you may buy whatever you would like to eat. Eat it in YHVH's presence. When you are feasting, do not forget to include the Levites. Remember, they have no inheritance.

At the end of every three years, bring that year's tithe and store it in your towns. Then the Levite, foreigner, fatherless, and widow will all have enough to eat. You will be blessed if you do this."

Discussion:

Where is an Israelite commanded to eat his tithe?

What should an Israelite do if he lives too far away to travel with his tithe?

Part IV: Deuteronomy 15:1-23

NT: Romans 6:15-23

"At the end of every seven years, every Israelite must forgive the debts of their fellow Israelites. There shouldn't be anyone living in Israel who is not taken care of. If you obey His commands, YHVH will bless you with more than enough.

If a fellow Israelite is poor, do not worry about giving to them thinking, 'Oh no! It's almost the seventh year, and I will have to forgive what they owe me.' If they cry out to God because you have not been generous, you will be guilty of sin. Give generously, and YHVH will bless you.

If any Israelite sells themselves to you as a servant, let them go free after six years of work. When you let them go free, send them with livestock and food. Remember, you were slaves in Egypt. If your servant does not want to go free after six years, he or she may choose to be your servant for life. Do not be upset if they decide to go free; you have been blessed with six years of service.

You should set aside your firstborn livestock and eat them in the place YHVH chooses to make holy. But only sacrifice the perfect animals. You may eat the other ones at home."

Discussion:

Why might someone feel less generous right before the seventh year?

Part V: Deuteronomy 16:1-17

NT: Luke 2:41-42; Mark 14:12-26

"Pay attention, and mark the month of Aviv: the first month of your year. Celebrate the Passover in the first month, because that is when YHVH brought you out of Egypt. Sacrifice the Passover in the evening in the place YHVH chooses. Do not sacrifice it in any other place. Roast it, and eat it in the place YHVH chooses. Do not eat the Passover with yeast, and do not leave any of the meal until morning. Eat unleavened bread for six more days to remind you that you left Egypt in a hurry. Come together on the seventh day for a holy day where you do not work.

Count seven weeks from the time you cut the grain. Then, celebrate the Feast of Weeks by bringing an offering to YHVH. If you have been blessed with a lot, bring a large offering. Praise YHVH in the place He will choose to put His Name.

After you have gathered the corn and wine harvest, celebrate the Feast of Tabernacles for seven days. Be joyful. YHVH will bless all the work you have done.

These are the three times a year that every Israelite man must come before YHVH in the place YHVH will choose: Unleavened Bread, the Feast of Weeks, and the Feast of Tabernacles. Each of you should bring an offering based on how YHVH has blessed you."

Discussion:

What details about these feast days can you remember (that are not mentioned in this passage)?

Shoftim (Judges) –
Deuteronomy 16:18 - 21:9; Isaiah 51:12 - 52:12

Portion:

Part I: Deuteronomy 16:18-17:20

NT: Matthew 18:15-17

"When YHVH gives you a new town to live in, set up judges and leaders for every tribe who will judge the people fairly. Do not accept a bribe or play favorites. Follow justice, and you will live in the land YHVH is giving you.

Do not set up Asherah poles or standing stones beside the altars you build to YHVH. YHVH hates those things.

Do not sacrifice an animal that is not perfect. YHVH is disgusted by this.

If you hear that someone in one of your towns is worshipping other gods or bowing to the sun, moon, or stars, find out if this is true. If it is, that person must die. But no one may be put to death unless two or three people witness against them, and the witnesses must be the first people to throw their stones at the guilty person.

If a local town judge is given a case that is too difficult for him, he should take that case to the Levitical priests and the judge who is in office at the time. You must do whatever the judge decides. Anyone who disobeys the judge will be put to death.

When you are living in the land that YHVH gives you, you will decide that you want a king like the nations around you have. Be careful to elect the man YHVH chooses. He must be an Israelite. He must not take large herds of horses for himself or take you back to Egypt to get more horses. He must not take many wives or store up much gold and silver for himself.

When he becomes king, he must write a copy of this Law, and he must keep it with him always. He is not above his fellow Israelites; the Law also applies to him. If he learns and follows the Law, his descendants will reign for a long time."

Discussion:

Why should the witnesses be the first to kill the guilty person?

Why shouldn't a wise king make himself very wealthy?

Part II: Deuteronomy 18:1-22

NT: Acts 3:13-26

"The Levitical priests and the whole tribe of Levi have no inheritance. The food offerings sacrificed to YHVH are theirs to eat. When a bull or a sheep is sacrificed, the shoulder, stomach, and meat from the head belong to the Levitical priests. The first of your grain, wine, olive oil, and wool belong to the priests because YHVH has chosen them to serve in His name.

If a Levite moves to the place where YHVH puts His name, that Levite may serve YHVH there. He may share in the tithes like the rest of the Levites do, even though he may have sold his possessions and made money before he began to serve YHVH.

When you enter the land, do not have anything to do with pagan practices. Let no Israelite ever be found sacrificing his children, fortune telling, practicing witchcraft, or talking to the spirits of dead people. Anyone who does these things is disgusting to YHVH. The pagan nations do these disgusting things, and that is why YHVH is driving them out of the land.

YHVH is allowing you to conquer the pagan people. They listen to fortune tellers, and they try to see into the future. You will not do these things. YHVH will bring another Prophet like me.

This Prophet will be an Israelite, and you will listen to Him. YHVH will speak through this Prophet because you said, 'Don't let God speak to us anymore or we will die!" YHVH agreed, and He is going to give you another Prophet like me. You must listen to everything He says, or God will deal with you. But you must kill any prophet who speaks things that God has not commanded or who speaks in the name of other gods.

If a prophet predicts things in the name of YHVH, and those things he predicts do not come true, then you know he has spoken without permission."

Discussion:

Pagan nations learn about their futures by seeking fortune tellers. How should an Israelite learn about things that will happen in the future?

At Sinai, the people asked YHVH not to speak directly to them anymore. What did YHVH decide?

Part III: Deuteronomy 19:1-21

NT: John 8:1-20

"When YHVH begins to give you the land and you live in the towns where your enemies used to live, set aside three towns as cities of refuge. Divide the land into three parts, and set up one city of refuge in each part. If someone kills someone else accidentally, they can run to the refuge that is closest to them. If the refuge was too far away, the victim's relative might catch the killer and kill him before the trial, so he must have a close place to run to. But if someone kills a person on purpose, they must be killed.

If YHVH continues to give you more land until He has given you all the land He promised to your ancestors, set aside three more cities of refuge so that no one will live too far from one.

Do not move your neighbor's boundary markers in the land YHVH is giving you.

One witness is not enough to convict someone of a crime. No one will be convicted unless two or three witnesses are willing to testify against them. If a witness lies because they are trying to get someone in trouble, the witness and the person on trial will both stand in front of the judge. The judge will investigate, and if he proves that the witness is a liar, the witness will receive the same punishment that was meant for the person on trial."

Discussion:

What do you think our courts and jails would look like if we followed Torah here today?

Part IV: Deuteronomy 20:1-20

NT: II Corinthians 4:7-15

"When you go to war, do not be afraid. YHVH, the God who brought you out of Egypt, will be with you. The priest will stand before the army and say, 'Do not be afraid.'

Then the officers will ask the soldiers, 'Has anyone built a new house? Has anyone planted a new vineyard? Has anyone become engaged to be married? If you have, then go home and enjoy these things so that someone else does not enjoy them instead of you.' The officers will also say, 'Is anyone afraid? If you are, go home so that you do not make the other soldiers afraid like you.'

When you march up to a city to attack it, first offer them peace. If they accept it, they may live as your servants. If they do not, kill all the men and spare the women and children. Take everything in the city for yourselves. Do not offer peace to the Hittites, Amorites, Canaanites, Perizzites, Hivites and Jebusites. Completely destroy them. If you don't destroy them, they will talk you into following their gods.

When you are in battle to capture a city, do not cut down all the trees. The trees are not your enemies; they are there for your benefit. Leave the fruit trees for food. You may cut down the others for building weapons and forts."

Discussion:

Why were certain men exempt from battle? Why were the fearful sent home?

Part V: Deuteronomy 21:1-9

NT: I Corinthians 4:4-5

"If a dead body is found in a field and no one knows who the killer is, find out which town is closest to the body. The elders from that town should take a young cow that has never been worked and lead it to a valley that has not been plowed or planted. They should lead it to a stream and break its neck. Then, the Levitical priests should step forward, and the town elders should wash their hands over the dead cow. When they do this, they should say, 'Our hands did not do this, and our eyes did not see it. Please clean us. Do not find us guilty of this murder since we have done what you asked us to do.'"

Discussion:

If there were no witnesses, the murderer could not be punished. How was the sin of murder dealt with then?

Ki Tetze (When you go out) –
Deuteronomy 21:10 - 25:19; Isaiah 54:1-13

Portion:

Part I: Deuteronomy 21:10-23

NT: Galatians 3:9-14

"When you go to war to defeat a nation, your men might find young women there that they want to marry. This is fine. An Israelite man may take a captured woman into his house to be his wife, but he may not marry her for thirty days. Have her shave her head, trim her nails, and change from the clothes she was wearing. If, after thirty days, the man still wants to marry her, then he may do so. If he has changed his mind, he must let her go. He may not treat her like a slave, because he has done her wrong.

If a man has two wives and he loves one wife more than the other, he may not treat the children of the loved wife better than the children of the unloved wife. The firstborn son should receive a double inheritance whether his mother is the loved wife or not.

If parents have a son who will not listen to them, who is rebellious, who eats too much, and who drinks until he is drunk, they should take him to the elders at the gate. The men of the town will stone him to death so that others will not follow his example.

If a guilty person is put to death, his body should be hanged from a tree. But do not leave his body there overnight; bury it the same day. Anyone hanged from a tree is cursed, and you must not make the land unholy; it is your inheritance from YHVH."

Discussion:

Why could the Israelite man not marry the captive woman right away? Why might he feel differently about her with her head shaved and her clothes changed?

Whose body was hanged on a tree because He was cursed for our sake?

Part II: Deuteronomy 22:1-30

NT: II Corinthians 6:14-15

"If you find an ox, a sheep, a jacket, a shirt, or anything that belongs to another Israelite, take it back to its owner. If the owner lives too far away or you do not know who the owner is, then take the thing you found to your house. Give it to the owners when they come to get it.

If you see that an animal has fallen on the road, do not pass by. Stop and help its owner to rescue it.

Women should not dress like men, and men should not dress like women.

When you find a bird's nest where a mother bird is sitting on her eggs or baby birds, you may take the babies. Do not take the mother. If you obey, you will be blessed and live a long life.

When you build a new house, build a wall around the roof. This way, you will not be made guilty by someone falling off.

Do not mix two kinds of seeds in your vineyard, or the plants and fruit will be polluted.

Do not plow with an ox and a donkey in one yoke.

Do not wear clothes made from wool mixed with linen.

Make tassels on the four corners of your clothing."

[Mature content ahead.]

"If a new husband claims that his wife has tricked him and that she was with another man before marrying him, he must take her to the elders at the gate. The elders will ask for proof, and they will find out whether or not the husband is right. If the husband is wrong about his wife, the elders will take him and discipline him. For as long as he lives, he will never be allowed to divorce her. But if it is proven that the wife lied to her husband, then she will be put to death.

If a man sleeps with another man's wife, they must both be stoned to death.

If a man sleeps with a young woman who is engaged to someone else, they must both be stoned to death.

If a man forces a married or engaged woman to sleep with him, he must be put to death. She has done nothing wrong.

If a man forces a young woman to sleep with him and she is not engaged to someone else, he must pay for the right to marry her. He can never divorce her for as long as he lives.

A man must never marry his father's wife."

Discussion:

What should an Israelite do if they find a donkey wandering down the road?

Israelites spent a lot of time on their flat roofs. What was every roof required to have for the sake of safety?

Part III: Deuteronomy 23:1-25

NT: II Corinthians 6:16-18

"No man whose male body part has been crushed or removed may enter the assembly of YHVH.

Children who come from a forbidden marriage may not enter the assembly—neither may any of their children up to ten generations later.

No Ammonite or Moabite, even ten generations later, may enter the assembly. They did not give you food and water when you came out of Egypt, and they tried to curse you by hiring Balaam. YHVH would not listen to Balaam, and He turned curses into blessings for you. For as long as you live, do not make a friendship agreement with these people.

Do not hate an Edomite; they are your relatives. Do not hate an Egyptian, because you lived in their land as strangers. These people may enter the assembly of YHVH in the third generation.

When you're at war, be sure to stay away from anything unclean and unholy. If an Israelite man becomes unclean in the night because of his dreams, he must leave the camp for the day. Then he may take a bath and come back.

Make sure there are specific bathroom spots outside the camp. When you go to use the bathroom, carry a shovel so that you can dig a hole and bury your waste. YHVH moves through the camp. Do not leave anything unclean lying around, or YHVH will turn away from you.

If a slave runs away and comes to live in your land, do not give him back to his master. Let him stay, and treat him well.

No Israelite man or woman may ever sleep with another person for money. No money earned in this way will be accepted by YHVH.

If you make a loan to an Israelite, do not charge him interest.

If you tell YHVH that you will do something, do it quickly. It's much better not to promise than to promise and not keep it.

You may pick grapes from your neighbor's vineyard but only as many as you can eat while you are there. You may not take any grapes with you. You may pick kernels of wheat from your neighbor's field, but you may not use tools to cut the stalks."

Discussion:

Who are the Edomites? How are they relatives of Israel?

What does it mean to charge interest on a loan?

Part IV: Deuteronomy 24:1-22

NT: Romans 7

"If a man divorces a woman and she marries another man, she may never go back to her first husband. This is something that YHVH hates.

If a man has just gotten married, he should be allowed to stay with his wife for the first year. He should not be sent to war or given work to do.

When you loan money to someone, you may take something of theirs (a pledge) to hold until they pay you back. Do not take something they need for their work.

Anyone caught kidnapping and selling Israelites as slaves will be put to death.

If someone has a skin disease, make sure and do exactly what the Levitical priests tell you to do. Remember what happened to Miriam.

When you loan money to someone, do not go into their house to find something to keep as a pledge. Let them bring something out to you. If they are so poor that they must give you their coat or robe, return it before night so that they will not be cold. YHVH will see your good deed.

Pay your employees right away. Do not take advantage of them. If they cry to YHVH because you have not been fair, you will be guilty.

Parents are not put to death for their children's sin, and children are not put to death for their parents' sin.

Do not mistreat the foreigner, the fatherless, or the widow. Remember, you were slaves in Egypt until YHVH rescued you. So, when you are harvesting, don't be careful to pick and gather everything. Don't go back and check again. Leave the extra harvest for the foreigner, the fatherless, and the widow."

Discussion:

What is a pledge? Why would someone take something from the person they loaned money to?

Farmers were required to leave the corners of their fields unharvested. What else were they required to do for the poor?

Part V: Deuteronomy 25:1-19

NT: Mark 12:18-27; I Corinthians 9:4-18

"If the judge decides that a person is guilty and deserves to be beaten, he must decide how many whips the person deserves and must watch as the person is whipped. He may not have the guilty person whipped more than forty times, however, because that is too humiliating.

Do not stop an ox from eating while it is working to grind the grain.

If two brothers are living together and one of them dies without having a son, the living brother should marry his brother's wife. He should give his brother a son so that his name will live on. If the man does not want to do this, the widow will go to the elders and tell them what has happened. If the man still refuses to marry her, she will disrespect him by taking one of his sandals, spitting in his face, and saying, 'This is what happens to a man who refuses to build his brother's family!' That man's family will be shamed.

If a woman tries to rescue her husband by grabbing the male parts of the man he is fighting with, you must cut off her hand.

Do not have dishonest weights so that you can cheat people in business deals. YHVH hates dishonest people.

Remember when the Amalekites attacked you as you came out of Egypt? They knew you were tired from the journey, and they did not fear YHVH. YHVH will erase them from the earth. Don't forget it!"

Discussion:

Why would someone have weights that were not honest? What does that mean?

Why did the judge need to watch as the guilty person was punished?

Ki Tavo (When you come in) – Deuteronomy 26:1 - 29:8; Isaiah 60:1-22

Portion:

Part I: Deuteronomy 26:1-15

NT: Acts 4:32-37

"When you have entered the Promised Land and have planted crops and harvested them, take some of the first fruits and put them in a basket. Take that basket to the place where YHVH has chosen to put His Name. Then say to the priest, 'I am here to say that I have come to the land YHVH swore to my fathers.'

Give the basket to the priest, and he will place it in front of the altar. Then say, 'My father was a wandering Aramean, and he went down to Egypt with his family. While in Egypt, my father's family became a large nation, but the Egyptians made us slaves. We cried to YHVH, and He heard us. He brought us out of Egypt with many miracles. He brought us to this land which flows with milk and honey. Now, to YHVH, I bring the first of what I have grown and harvested from this land.' After you have said this, you, the Levites, and all the foreigners with you will feast before YHVH.

The third year is the year of the tithe. In the third year, you will set aside a tenth of your harvest so that the Levites, the foreigner, the fatherless, and the widow will all have enough to eat. After you have obeyed this command, you will say to YHVH, 'I have given away the set-aside food just as you commanded. I did not eat any of it, I did not touch it while I was unclean, and I have not offered any of it to the dead. I have obeyed You. Look down from Your Holy House and bless Israel and the Promised Land.' "

Discussion:

Why were the Israelites supposed to remember where they came from while giving the first of their harvest to YHVH?

Why were the Israelites supposed to give away a tenth of their third-year harvest?

Part II: Deuteronomy 26:16-27:8

NT: II John 1:4-6

"On this day, YHVH commands you to carefully remember and obey everything He has said. He calls you His treasured possession, and you are to obey Him. He says that He will give you a great reputation. You will be honored above all other nations just as He promised."

Moses and the elders spoke to the people of Israel. They said, "Keep every command that I give you today. When you cross the Jordan to enter the land, set up large stones. Set up these stones on Mount Ebal, and cover the stones with plaster. Build an altar to YHVH, and do not use any iron tools when you build it. Offer burned offerings there. Sacrifice fellowship offerings, and eat and praise YHVH together. Write all the words of this Law on the stones that you covered in plaster."

Discussion:

Where were the Israelites commanded to build an altar?

What were the Israelites commanded to write on the stones covered in plaster?

Part III: Deuteronomy 27:9-26

NT: Ephesians 5:1-14

Then Moses and the Levitical priests said to all the people of Israel, "Be quiet and listen! You have now become the people of YHVH. Follow His commands."

Moses said, "After you have crossed the Jordan, the tribes of Simeon, Levi, Judah, Issachar, Joseph, and Benjamin will stand on Mount Gerizim to bless the people. The tribes of Reuben, Gad, Asher, Zebulun, Dan, and Naphtali will stand on Mount Ebal to speak the curses.

The Levites will say:

'Cursed is anyone who makes an idol,' and the people will agree.

'Cursed is anyone who dishonors his parents,' and the people will agree.

'Cursed is anyone who moves his neighbor's boundary,' and the people will agree.

'Cursed is anyone who tricks the blind,' and the people will agree.

'Cursed is anyone who mistreats the foreigner, fatherless, or widow,' and the people will agree.

'Cursed is anyone who sleeps with his father's wife the way a man sleeps with his own wife,' and the people will agree.

'Cursed is anyone who sleeps with an animal the way a man sleeps with his wife,' and the people will agree.

'Cursed is anyone who sleeps with his sister the way a man sleeps with his wife,' and the people will agree.

'Cursed is anyone who sleeps with his mother-in-law the way a man sleeps with his wife,' and the people will agree.

'Cursed is anyone who kills his neighbor on purpose,' and the people will agree.

'Cursed is anyone who is paid to kill an innocent person,' and the people will agree.

'Cursed is anyone who disobeys the Law,' and the people will agree."

Discussion:

What two mountains did YHVH choose as the places where the Israelites would speak the curses and the blessings?

Part IV: Deuteronomy 28:1-14

NT: Matthew 5

"If you obey all the commands of YHVH, then He will make you blessed above all nations on Earth. These are the blessings you will enjoy if you obey YHVH:

You will be blessed in the city and blessed in the country.

Your children will be blessed, your crops will be blessed, and your livestock will be blessed. You will have plenty of bread to eat.

You will be blessed when you leave and blessed when you arrive.

Your enemies will be defeated, and they will run from you.

YHVH will bless your barns and all your work. He will bless you in the Promised Land. If you obey all His commands, He will make you His holy people. He will make you prosper in the Promised Land.

YHVH will send rain from heaven to bless your crops. You will lend to many nations, but you will never need to borrow. He will make you a leader and not a follower. Pay attention to all the commands of YHVH. Do not follow other gods."

Discussion:

What will ensure the blessing of YHVH in the Promised Land? What must the people do in order to be blessed?

Part V: Deuteronomy 28:15-29:8

NT: Matthew 25:40-42; Revelation 16:1-11

"However, if you disobey the commands of YHVH, if you are not careful to follow them all, these are the curses that will come into your lives:

You will be cursed in the city and cursed in the country.

You will not have enough bread to eat.

Your children will be cursed, your crops will be cursed, and your livestock will be cursed. You will be cursed when you leave and cursed when you arrive.

Everything you do will be cursed until you are destroyed. YHVH will send plagues until you are wiped from the land. He will send unbearable heat and drought. The sky will not send rain, and the soil will not grow crops until you are completely destroyed.

YHVH will allow your enemies to defeat you, and you will run from them. Your dead bodies will be food for wild animals and birds. YHVH will send the diseases of Egypt as well as madness, blindness, and confusion. You will stumble, and nothing you do will prosper. You will be robbed, and no one will rescue you.

You will be engaged to a woman, but another man will take her. You will build a house, but you will not live in it. You will plant a vineyard, but you will never enjoy it. Your animals will be killed in front of you, but you will not eat the meat. Your sons and daughters will be sold as slaves, and all these things will cause you to lose your mind.

YHVH will drive you out of the Promised Land, and in foreign lands you will worship other gods. The other nations will make fun of you and look down on you.

You will plant and plant, but your harvest will be small. Worms and locusts will eat from your fields and vineyards. The olives will fall from the trees before you can use them.

The foreigners living in your land will begin to rule over you. They will be above you, and you will have to borrow from them.

All these curses will come to you if you do not obey YHVH's commands. They will be a sign to you and to your descendants forever that because you did not serve YHVH when things were good, He sent these curses against you.

He will bring a cruel nation to destroy you. They will leave you with nothing. You will be so hungry that you will eat your own children.

He will even bring diseases against you that are not written in this Book of the Law. Just as YHVH made you great, so He will destroy you. He will scatter you to the ends of the earth where you will worship other gods and live miserable lives where you are constantly afraid. You will try to sell yourselves as slaves, but no one will buy you."

These are the rules of the covenant that YHVH commanded Moses to make with the Israelites in Moab in addition to the covenant YHVH had made with the people at Horeb.

Moses said to the Israelites, "You saw what YHVH did to Pharaoh, but to this day YHVH has not given you eyes to see or a mind to truly understand. Now, YHVH wants you to see that for forty years He has led you through the wilderness. Your clothes and your sandals have not worn out. You have eaten only manna—not bread or fermented drink. He's done this so that you will know YHVH is God.

When we reached this place, Sihon king of Heshbon and Og king of Bashan came out to fight us, but we took their land and gave it to the tribe of Rueben, the tribe of Gad, and the half-tribe of Manasseh."

Discussion:

Obedience brings blessing. What does disobedience bring?

Nitzavim (Standing) –
Deuteronomy 29:9 - 30:20; Isaiah 61:10 - 63:9

Vayelech (He went) –
Deuteronomy 31:1-30; Micah 7:18-20;
Joel 2:15-27; Hosea 14:2-10

(In leap years these portions are read separately.)

Portion:

Part I: Deuteronomy 29:9-29

NT: Hebrews 12:1-17

"Be careful to follow the rules of this covenant that God is making with you and also with your children who will be born after you. We are standing in front of Him today and agreeing to be His people so that He can keep the promise He made to Abraham, Isaac, and Jacob.

You remember the gods of Egypt and the gods of the people we passed on our way here. Make sure no one in Israel follows these other gods. If they do, they will be like a root that poisons the whole plant with bitter poison. These people think they can have the blessings of this agreement without obeying the rules, but YHVH will curse them with all the curses.

Your grandchildren will look at the terrible curses, and all the nations will say, 'Why has YHVH cursed the land? Why is He so angry?' He will have done this because His people walked away from their agreement. Because they walked away and followed other gods, He cursed them with the curses of the agreement and kicked them out of the land. But YHVH has shown us His secrets so that we can follow Him forever."

Discussion:

If some of the people start to follow other gods, what does Moses say will happen to the rest of Israel?

Some people listen to the blessings, but they do not think the curses will ever happen to them? What does Moses say about this?

What does it mean to follow other gods? Does it always mean that someone is bowing down and worshipping an idol?

Part II: Deuteronomy 30:1-10

NT: Romans 2:1-16

"When you and your children are sorry because of all the curses in your life, and when you begin to obey YHVH with all your heart, He will bring you back to the Promised Land. No matter how far He has sent you, He will bring you back. He will bless you even more than He blessed your fathers. He will circumcise your hearts so that you can love Him with everything you are. The curses that were on you will be on your enemies. He will bless everything that you do. He will bless your children and your animals and your crops. If you obey Him with your whole heart and soul, it will make Him happy to bless you."

Discussion:

If YHVH's people repent after they are cursed, what will God do?

Part III: Deuteronomy 30:11-20

NT: Galatians 6:1-10; I John 5:2-4

"These instructions are not too difficult for you. They are in your mouth and heart so that you can obey them. I am giving you a choice between life and blessing or death and destruction. Love YHVH; obey everything that He says, and He will give you incredible blessings in the Promised Land.

If you disobey, if you turn to other gods, you will be destroyed. You will not be allowed to stay in the Promised Land. Your choice is between life and death. You have a choice to be blessed or to be cursed. Choose life. If you do, you and your children will live as obedient people. You will hold on to YHVH because He is your life. He will give you long lives in the land He promised to Abraham, Isaac, and Jacob."

Discussion:

What two choices does Moses give the people?

Why would anyone choose to be cursed? Have you ever made a choice that you knew would not work out for your best?

Part IV: Deuteronomy 31:1-8

NT: Colossians 1:1-14

Moses said to the people, "I am one hundred and twenty years old. I am too old to lead you anymore. YHVH has told me that I will not cross the Jordan; He will cross ahead of you. He will destroy your enemies, and you will live in their land. Joshua will also cross ahead of you. YHVH will do to your enemies what He did to Sihon and Og. You must do to them exactly what I have said. Be strong, and don't be scared. YHVH is with you, and He will never leave you."

In front of all the Israelites, Moses spoke to Joshua. He said, "Be strong. Don't be afraid. You must lead Israel into the Promised Land, and you must divide the land for the people. Give each tribe their inheritance. YHVH is with you, and He will never leave you."

Discussion:

Moses told the people that YHVH would destroy Israel's enemies. Did that mean that they wouldn't need to fight?

Part V: Deuteronomy 31:9-30

NT: Matthew 7:21-27

Moses wrote down the laws that he had just spoken to the people. Then he gave them to the priests and the elders. He said, "At the end of every seven years, when the debts are being cancelled, read this to the people during the Feast of Sukkot. Read it to the men, the women, the children, and the foreigners who live in Israel. Then everyone can learn to fear YHVH and obey His laws."

YHVH said to Moses, "You are about to die. Get Joshua, and bring him to the Tabernacle with you." Moses did, and YHVH came to the door in a pillar of cloud. YHVH said, "You are going to die, and the Israelites will soon have relationships with other gods. They will turn their backs on Me, and they will not follow our agreement. Then, I will be angry, and I will turn My back on them. Many terrible things will happen to them, and they will know that I am not with them.

Write down this song, and teach it to the Israelites. It will witness against them. When I have brought them into the good land that I promised to their fathers, they will have more than enough to eat. Then, they will turn to other gods and break our agreement. When the terrible curses come, this song will testify against them. Their children will remember this song because I know what they are planning to do even before I take them into the land."

Moses wrote down the song and taught it to the Israelites.

YHVH said to Joshua, "Be strong, and don't be afraid. You will bring the people into the Promised Land, and I will be with you."

When Moses had finished writing down the Law, he gave the book to the Levites who carried the ark. He said, "Put this Book of the Law next to the Ark of the Covenant. It will be a witness against you. If you have been this rebellious while I have been leading you, how much worse will you be after I die! Bring all the elders to me so I can say these things to them. Heaven and Earth will testify against you if you do not keep the rules of your agreement with YHVH. Disaster will come because you will make YHVH very angry."

Discussion:

What kind of song was Moses told to teach the people?

Is Moses concerned about how the people will act after he is dead?

Ha'azinu (Hear) – Deuteronomy 32:1-52; II Samuel 22:1-51

Portion:

Part I: Deuteronomy 32:1-9

NT: Revelation 15

This is the song that Moses taught the people:

"Hear, heavens. Listen, Earth. My words will fall like rain on the grass. I will speak the name of YHVH. Praise Him because He is great! He is a rock. He is perfect and fair; He is always faithful.

Those who do evil are not His children. They are shamed. Is this the way you pay Him back for all His kindness? You are fools! Isn't He the Creator who made you?

Remember the old days; ask your parents and grandparents to tell you about them. Ask them about when the Most High God divided the land as an inheritance for the sons of Israel."

Discussion:

To whom is Moses singing these words? Why?

Part II: Deuteronomy 32:10-21

NT: Romans 10:14-21

"He found them in a desert, and He took care of them. He guarded them like a treasure: like the apple of His eye. He protected them like a mother eagle protects her young. YHVH led Israel by Himself; He did not have the help of any false gods.

He fed Israel with the best things from the land: fruit, honey, bread, meat, and wine. Israel was fat and well-fed. Then, they abandoned the God who made them a nation. They rejected the Rock, their Savior.

They went to other gods, and they made God jealous. They sacrificed to new gods who had given them nothing. They forgot the God who gave them everything.

YHVH saw this, and He was angry. He said, 'I will hide from them, and they will come to an end. They rejected Me to chase worthless idols. I will use people who are not a nation to make them jealous. I will use an unwise nation to make them angry.' "

Discussion:

What does God say He will do when His people make Him jealous?

Part III: Deuteronomy 32:22-31

NT: Hebrews 12:28-29

" 'My anger will light a raging fire. It will burn everything from the pit to the mountains. I will send them trouble, and I will destroy them with disease. I will send animals and people to kill them—from the young to the old. I said I would scatter them and destroy them, but I did not want their enemies to think that they had won.'

Israel does not understand. I wish they did! One person cannot chase a thousand people unless YHVH is with him. Our enemies' gods are not like Israel's God; even our enemies understand this."

Discussion:

Israel should know that God is with them. Why?

Part IV: Deuteronomy 32:32-43

NT: Romans 12:14-19

"Their vines come from Sodom, and their fields are like Gomorrah. Their grapes are full of poison.

YHVH says, 'I have been saving up their punishment, and I will pay back those who do wrong. I am the one who pays back for wrongs. Their day of punishment is coming soon.'

YHVH will defend His people. When He sees that their strength is gone, He will have mercy on them. He will say, 'Why aren't your gods protecting you? Let them help you! Now you will see that I am the only God. I kill and bring back to life. I have wounded, and now I will heal. I will sharpen My sword, and I will pay back My enemies. I will pay back everyone who hates Me.'

Be happy, because He will have revenge for the blood of His people. He will repay His enemies, and He will make things right for His people and His land."

Discussion:

What does YHVH plan to do after He's allowed the enemies to defeat His people?

Part V: Deuteronomy 32:44-52

NT: Philippians 3:17-21

Moses stood with Joshua and spoke all these words to the people. When he'd finished, he said, "These words are very serious. They are not just words; they will let you live. If you remember them, you will live long lives in the Promised Land."

That same day, YHVH told Moses to climb Mount Nebo across from Jericho. He said, "Climb the mountains, and look at Canaan. On that mountain, you will die just like Aaron died on Mount Hor. You will not enter the land because you did not honor Me in front of the people when you were in Meribah. I will let you see the land from a distance."

Discussion:

Why is Moses only allowed to see Canaan from a distance?

V'Zot HaBrachah (This is the blessing) – Deuteronomy 33:1 - 34:12; Joshua 1:1-18

Portion:

Part I: Deuteronomy 33:1-5

NT: Matthew 24:30-32

Before Moses died, he blessed the people of Israel. He said, "YHVH came from Mount Sinai. He rose like the sun, and He showed His great power. YHVH so loves His people. He cares for everyone who belongs to Him. They bow at His feet, and He teaches them through Moses. YHVH became King of Israel, and Israel gathered together."

Discussion:

Who did YHVH use to teach the people?

Part II: Deuteronomy 33:6-17

NT: Hebrews 11:21

"Let Reuben live, and let his men be counted.

YHVH, listen to Judah. Bring him to his people. Help him against his enemies!

Your Thummim and Urim belong to Levi. You tested him, and he chose You above his family. He teaches Your laws to Israel, and he burns incense and offerings on Your altar.

Benjamin is loved by YHVH. He rests on God's chest and is protected by Him.

YHVH, bless Joseph with rain and deep wells and the best things of the land. Let the favor of the One from the burning bush rest on Joseph's head. He is a prince among his brothers."

Discussion:

How are these blessings different/the same from the blessings of Jacob over his sons?

Part III: Deuteronomy 33:18-25

NT: I Peter 1:1-5

"Zebulun, be blessed in your travels. Issachar, be blessed at home. Zebulun and Issachar will call people to the mountain to offer the right sacrifices. They will make their living from the sea.

Whoever gives Gad land will be blessed. Gad lives like a lion. Gad has done right and has judged Israel fairly.

Dan is like a lion cub.

YHVH is especially kind to Naphtali.

Asher is the most blessed of all his brothers. He will be strong for as long as he lives."

Discussion:

How are these blessings different/the same from the blessings of Jacob over his sons?

Part IV: Deuteronomy 33:26-29

NT: Romans 11:1-5

"There is no one like Israel's God. He rides through the skies to rescue you. Underneath the wings of the everlasting God is your safe place. He will chase your enemies and say to you, 'Destroy them!' And so Israel will be safe in a land with plenty to eat. You are so blessed, Israel. No one in the whole world is as blessed as you to be saved by YHVH. He is your shield and your sword. Your enemies will run from you."

Discussion:

What about Israel is different from the rest of the world?

Part V: Deuteronomy 34:1-12

NT: II Corinthians 3:7-18

Moses climbed Mount Nebo, and he looked down at the land. YHVH showed him the whole land from Gilead to Dan: Naphtali's land, Ephraim and Manasseh's land, the land of Judah to the Mediterranean Sea, the Negev, and the Valley of

Jericho as far as Zoar. YHVH said, "This is the land I promised to Abraham, Isaac, and Jacob's descendants. You may see it with your eyes, but you may not cross into it."

So Moses died there, and he was buried in Moab. To this day, no one knows where his grave is. Moses was one hundred and twenty years old when he died, but he still had his eyesight and his strength. The Israelites mourned for Moses for thirty days.

Joshua was filled with the spirit of wisdom because Moses had laid his hands on him. The Israelites listened to Joshua. They obeyed what YHVH had told them through Moses.

Since then, there hasn't been a prophet in Israel like Moses who YHVH knew face to face. No one has shown the power of YHVH like Moses did in front of all of Israel.

Discussion:

How old was Moses when he died?

Who buried Moses?

Where did Moses die?

www.ingramcontent.com/pod-product-compliance
Lightning Source LLC
Chambersburg PA
CBHW070733170426
43200CB00007B/511